DREAM JOB:
Redefined

The New Rules for Creating a Career That Matters and Doing Work You Love

By Mitch Matthews

D0920876

Copyright © 2018 Mitch Matthews

All rights reserved. No part of this publication may be reproduced, distributed, or transmitted in any form or by any means, including photocopying, recording, or other electronic or mechanical methods, without the prior written permission of the author, except in the case of brief quotations embodied in reviews and certain other non-commercial uses permitted by copyright law.

ISBN-13: 978-0-9909659-1-6

www.mitchmatthews.com

Cover Design by Ida Fia Sveningsson
(www.idafiasveningsson.se)

Cover Photo by Justin Salem Meyer
(http://www.justinsalemmeyer.com)

Author Coach: Lise Cartwright
(https://www.hustleandgroove.com)

GRAB YOUR FREE GIFT!

DREAM JOB:

WORKBOOK

As a thank you for purchasing my book, I'd love to give you access to the companion workbook.

This workbook is designed to be used as you read through the book and provides you with all the coaching questions and journal areas you need.

Claim your FREE copy here: https:// www.mitchmatthews.com/DJRworkbook

Table of Contents

Introduction

I can remember thinking, "What have I done?"

I had taken a job right out of college. It was the first one offered.

The idea of it was pretty darn glamorous... at least to me. I would be in the "Executive Leadership Development Program" of a national department store chain.

Yup.

The E.L.D.P.

I was supposed to be on the fast track to a high-level leadership position. It meant exposure to all areas of the organization and it was supposed to mean I'd be learning from the best.

There would be travel.

There would be training.

Opportunities would abound.

Oh yeah. It sounded pretty sweet.

I was a bit of a goober as I bragged to my friends about it. I threw in mentions of possible trips to Europe to check out trends... getting to meet with top execs on a regular basis... and freakishly cool offices downtown.

But within two hours of my first day, I was struck by a sinking feeling.

After a quick tour and a promise of a more "robust" orientation in the days to come, I was escorted to my cubical.

I was told I'd share it with Matt, a "Two-Year Graduate of the E.L.D.P."

As I entered my new shared space, Matt looked up at me with the dull eyes of a prisoner on death row. He nodded and then returned to enter more data into a spreadsheet. My tour guide informed me Matt would be "showing me the ropes" until my E.L.D.P. classes kicked into high gear.

Then... like a department store ninja... she disappeared around the corner.

As I slid into the worn office chair next to my "cellmate," a feeling of dread washed over me. From where I sat... I could see over the short cubical walls. Each pod seemed to have a different version of a Matt. Some were the same age, but others were 5, 10, or 20 years older.

No one seemed to be smiling.

No one seemed to be engaged.

No one seemed to be loving their work.

I tried to smile and stay positive... but then my mind time-jumped.

I couldn't help but imagine myself in Matt's shoes... just a few years down the road.

Grumpy. Stressed. Grey.

Yikes.

I was quickly brought back to the present as Matt tossed me a manila folder and started to instruct me on how to enter numbers in the company's order tracking system.

As the first few days wore on, I saw more of the same. With each passing hour, I felt like I'd voluntarily stepped into a life sentence.

I felt trapped.

I felt stuck.

Then it happened.

Not immediately.

But gradually.

I started to think of people who were doing work they loved.

Marty... the owner of the bike shop I'd worked at growing up.

Mr. Mullen... my high school speech teacher.

My mom... who had gone back to school in her 30s and became a C.F.O. of a small manufacturing company in my hometown.

They didn't love their work in some "rainbows and butterflies" kind of way. They didn't run through the meadow singing songs as they headed to their job... as if they were in a Disney movie. (At least I don't think a little birdie ever landed on my mom's finger as she sang to it at her desk.)

But they loved their work.

As I thought about people like them... a fire started in my belly.

I began to study the idea of finding work you love.

That fascination turned into an obsession.

Little did I know it would eventually turn into my life's work.

Stifled in that little cubicle, I couldn't have imagined I would some day conduct 100s of interviews with people who love their work and love their lives. I would get to ask them how they did it.

We'd explore mindsets, systems, and processes.

I had no idea that those same interviews would become the backbone of my Huffington Post #1 rated podcast called: DREAM THINK DO and be downloaded by hundreds of thousands of people around the world.

[Check out the podcast at: www.MitchMatthews.com]

Nope.

When I was sitting there wondering if I'd be stuck in the same rut many of my E.L.D.P. counterparts seemed to be... I didn't have a clue I'd wind up utilizing the systems and the concepts we'll cover in this book to help coach thousands of people around the world to find work that mattered and create a life they loved.

I had no idea.

Heck, it would have been hard for me to even imagine as I sat there next to Matt entering data... that I would eventually have a crazy dream of wanting to help launch a million dreams in my lifetime.

But that happened too.

I know... I know.

THAT goal might sound a little weird. But since the idea of inspiring a million people to achieve dreams hatched in my heart, I've been driven by it. It helped me line up my passion and my purpose and it has energized me. It's also a key part of our "BIG Dream Gathering" movement. These are events we hold at top universities around the country where we invite students, faculty, and members of the local community to come dream big together.

It might sound a little braggadocious to say... but these events are amazing to experience. Not because of anything I do... but because it's a pure taste of heaven to see people giving themselves permission to dream and then helping each other to achieve those dreams. (More on all of this later.)

Even though I didn't know any of that "good stuff" was coming... even though I was sitting in that squeaky, faded office chair--waiting for my E.L.D.P. classes to start--I decided.

I decided I wasn't going to get stuck there.

I started to make small changes.

I began to experiment.

I committed.

Because that's what we have to do... right?

We have to decide it's possible.

We have to decide we're going to find work that we love... work that matters.

[NOTE: Some might consider us crazy, but hey, it's the crazies who change the world for the better.]

That's what I want for you!

I want you to find or create a career that you love.

Through this book, we're going to offer you a process to do that.

To that end... here's the quick scoop on where we're headed.

It's based on real-life stuff... my own experiences, hundreds of interviews, thousands of coaching sessions and the tens of thousands of people touched by the BIG Dream Gatherings.

Through all of this, we've been able to nail down a process that has helped countless people find or create Dream Jobs... in the real world.

A - ATTITUDE

You have to decide to choose the right attitude.
We'll talk about how to do it. But it's key.

B - BRIDGE

Not every job is going to be a "Dream Job."
You'll need to take a "Bridge Job" once in a while.

The key is to learn how to use the M.E.A.L. Plan™ to find the right job for this season of your life. As you do... you'll be able to get unstuck and move forward with confidence.

C - CLUES

You can look for "clues" in your past and present to get clarity on where you want to go in the future.

I'll walk you through specific strategies to help you identify the clues around you.

NOTE: If you're feeling a little stuck right now... this process will help you to get unstuck and start to get the momentum you've been longing for.

D - DREAM

We need to set goals for our career, but we also need to broaden our perspective and think about what we want to do, achieve and experience in LIFE too.

In fact, one of the consistent truths I uncovered through interviewing countless people who were in their Dream Jobs was they had thought about the "total package." They had set goals for their work... but they'd also dreamed about what they wanted their life to look like.

As a result, many had found work that helped them achieve and experience more of what they wanted at work... AND at home.

For some that meant finding work that allowed them to help people, for others it meant traveling the globe, and for others it meant fun stuff like extreme swimming or designing freakishly cool customized costumes for kids in wheelchairs.

Listen in to these episodes for the full story on each example:

- Helping others: www.MitchMatthews.com/131
- Travel: www.MitchMatthews.com/135
- Extreme Swimming:
  www.MitchMatthews.com/014
- Costumes for kiddos in wheelchairs:
  www.MitchMatthews.com/049

We have to give ourselves permission to dream, even when we feel unclear or feel like our dreams are on the ropes.

The key is to have specific strategies to help make this easier.

E - EXPERIMENT

There is power in "experimenting."

Try things. Be curious. Learn.
Give yourself permission to be an "amateur" at something for a while... without the pressure of having to "go pro" with it.

Uncover and discover more of what you were put on the planet to do.

[We'll cover how to do this effectively too.]

F - FAIL

Admittedly... as a "recovering perfectionist" myself... this was one of the toughest lessons for me to learn. But it was critical.

It's the idea that sometimes things aren't going to go the way we expect/want them to.

Sometimes things are going to "fail."

But that's okay.

The key is to know how to "fail like a scientist."

[We'll show you how to do that too.]

G - GOALS

Amid the clue-finding, dreaming, and experimenting, we also need to learn how to properly and effectively set goals.

Not in a New-Years-Resolutions-write-out-a-list-but-forget-them-in-48-hours-kind-of-way.

Nope.

We need a process to help you define your goals and build a plan in a compelling way so that they become "magnetic."

I'll be sharing that with you too!

H - HELP

We all need help.

The key is in HOW we ask and WHO we ask. Thanks to the era we live in... there are ways to get help previous generations never had.

We'll cover that too.

I - INTENTIONALITY

A majority of people don't like the work they do... day in and day out.

It's the norm.

It shouldn't be.

Intentionality is the linchpin to breaking free from this "my job sucks" norm... and finding work you love.

So we'll give you strategies so you can be more intentional... about being intentional. (Yeah, I said that.)

J - JOB(S)

This one is so subtle... I almost missed it.

But the "s" is the key.

Now... it's not about finding ONE job.

It's bigger than that.

It's about putting together a DREAM Career.

That's right. As I interviewed people who had

achieved Dream Jobs, almost every one of them had a consistent theme running through their lives.

It was that they had let go of the thought of finding ONE (singular) Dream Job.

Instead, they had worked to achieve a "dream career."

Gone are the days of finding that ONE job that will be the end-all-be-all job the rest of your life.

[NOTE: I'm not sure if this ever really existed. In fact, I think this concept is what has led to a lot of the cynicism that exists around the concept of a "Dream Job." The thought that once you were in a Dream Job, you'd never have a problem or feel like you were working at all.]

That's not what I'm talking about when I talk about Dream Jobs.

Plus... there's the idea of finding ONE company you would work for the entirety of your career. That used to exist. In fact, when my Grandpa Matthews returned from WWII, he signed on with John Deere and he worked there until he retired.

This was more of the norm for his generation.

But as you well know... that's not the norm any more.

And it's not what we're talking about with Dream Job Redefined either.

NOPE.

The people I talked with had set their sights on either creating or finding work they loved.

But they also knew that work would cause them to grow, evolve, and stretch.

As a result... the Dream Job for one season of their life might eventually become a Bridge Job and help them to move into a different Dream Job in the future.

That didn't mean they were flakey or inconsistent.

The people I spoke with were constantly bringing excellence in what they did. They were doing work that mattered. But they also were staying open to new things and continuing to push themselves.

So it wasn't so much about finding ONE job that would satisfy them the rest of their lives. Instead, it was about putting a series of JOBS together... to intentionally make for a DREAM CAREER.

Which brought me to the idea of Dream Job Redefined.

That's right.

Based on the research, interviews, and experiences, I've begun to define a Dream Job as:

dream·job

drēm\ \ˈjäb\

noun

Definition of Dream Job

1: Doing work you love

2: And/or doing work that enables you to do something you love

NOTE: This definition does NOT include any of the following:
1.) The work is always easy.
2.) The work only involves nice people.
3.) The work never involves risk.
4.) You don't have to work hard to achieve it.

Nope.

Dream Jobs still take work. You'll still come across "jackweeds" and mean people when you're in Dream Jobs. Dream Jobs still involve taking chances sometimes. And... Dream Jobs won't just be handed to you.

But YOU know this.

That's why you're reading a book like this.

I'm guessing that you might not be in a Dream Job right now.

But I'd also bet that your heart longs to be doing work you feel connected to... work where you can go "all in." Work that matters.

And/or... you're passionate about something outside of work... a group of people... a way of life... a sense of adventure... a cause bigger than you... and you have a sense deep down inside that although you LOVE this thing... whatever it is... you might not be able to make a career out of it... BUT you still feel called to it. So you want to find a job that will allow you to do do that thing you love outside of work.

Well... either way... whether it's the work itself... or something the work allows you to do... you want a Dream Job.

AND... I'm guessing... you are willing to work to achieve it.

Am I right?

If not, that's cool. Feel free to put this book down. Walk away.

Know that about 75% of the American workforce is either unemployed, unsatisfied, or underemployed. So although it pains me to say it... the "norm" is to NOT be in a Dream Job.

BUT... I can tell you, if you choose to keep reading... and more importantly, if you choose to apply the concepts we'll be exploring on the pages to come... you'll be on track to creating a Dream Career.

Finding or creating work you love.

Doing things that matter.

Living more of the life you were put on the planet to live.

A life of purpose.

A life of adventure.

A life of giving.

A life of fun.

Sound good?

I hope so.

By the way... deep down... you might be wondering how I can make this type of promise.

It's because over the past decade, I've seen this system work. I've seen the patterns time and time again in the people I've interviewed who either created or achieved their dream work.

Plus, I've shared these strategies with people who went from hating their jobs to finding and creating careers they now love.

And... I was able to use it too.

In fact, to wrap up this chapter... let's revisit that drab cubicle and the infamous E.L.D.P...

As you might have imagined, after a short season of feeling stuck and licking my wounds, I started to change. I began to apply some of the concepts we'll be talking about... even back then.

Within 3 months, I'd quit and found the perfect "Bridge Job" for that season of my life. It helped me move to a dream location (Montana) and eventually (within 2 years) score a Dream Job for that season of my life.

I didn't stop there. I kept learning and applying these concepts and I'm wildly grateful to say that it's helped me to achieve a Dream Career.

Sure... there have been some ups and downs. That's life.

But I've been able to find work-I've loved to do.

And... I've helped others to do it too.

Time and time again.

I want that for you.

I want you doing work you love and/or doing work that allows you to do something you love.

And... hey... I'm honored to be on this journey with you. To help you to find or create the work you love. Work that matters to you.

So... since you're still reading... I assume you're still

"in."

I'm glad.

I'm stoked... in fact.

Let's get to it.

NOTES:

Chapter One

A - ATTITUDE

This chapter can be short because I know you get it.

You're smart. I don't have to tell you this. I'm betting you're already with me. You know... deep down... that the new rules... the ways to create or find work you love... start with choosing the right attitude.

> *"Attitude is a little thing that makes a big difference."*
> - Winston Churchill

If you are going to find or create Dream Jobs, you have to decide to do it and then choose the right attitude as you move forward. We're not talking about rainbows-and-butterflies-and-everything-is-always-going-to-be-easy-if-we-just-pursue-our-passions type attitudes.

Nope. That's not us. That's not what we're talking about.

> "Nothing can stop the person with the right mental attitude from achieving their goal; nothing on earth can help the person with the wrong attitude."
> - Thomas Jefferson

I'm not going to spend too much time on this subject because if you're reading this book, there's a VERY good chance that you understand this. Your attitude matters.

> "The greatest discovery of all time is that a person can change their future by merely changing their attitude."
> - Oprah Winfrey

But let's also be real. If you've picked up this book, there's a strong possibility that your attitude has taken some hits lately.

- Maybe you're getting close to graduating but you're not sure what your next steps should be.
- Maybe you're in a "bad fit" job. You know it's not necessarily a bad job. It's just not a good

fit for you. BUT you're also starting to feel stuck. You're worried this is "as good as it gets."

- Maybe you've got a total "jackweed" for a boss. You work hard every day but that jerkwater of a manager doesn't appreciate you or your efforts.
- Maybe you've been in your career for a while and you're wondering if you screwed up. You hear that famous quote credited to Albert Einstein, and you're starting to identify with the fish. (The quote is: "Everyone is a genius. But if you judge a fish by its ability to climb a tree, it will live its whole life believing that it is stupid.") Amen?

This is tough stuff. I'll be the last one to tell you it isn't. I've been in these situations (each of them). So have the countless people I've interviewed. Don't worry. I'm not going to tell you to "buck up, lil' camper." Nope. That's not where we're headed.

We're going to plot a new course. Starting today.

One that's built on hundreds of interviews with people who've created dream careers.

Individuals who've persevered to find or create work that matters.

They've found work they love.

I want this for YOU too.

I think it's possible. No, I know it's possible. I won't say there won't be tough days mixed in. I'll tell you there will be rough times even when you're in your next Dream Job. Heck, one of the most common aspects I found in interviewing all these people is there is still something we labeled the "Suck Factor" in any job. I don't say this to be a downer. I just acknowledge it because I'm committed to shooting straight with you.

There are still going to be things you don't love to do... even when you find work you love.

For example, I LOVE the work I do. I love it.

But part of the "Suck Factor" of my job is accounting. I know it's a vital part of my business. I know you've got to make the debits and credits work to keep your doors open. I understand it. I respect it. I work hard at it. I just don't LOVE to spend time on it.

As our business has grown, I've been able to find great people to help me with it. But I still have to spend some time on it. It's necessary.

I don't love it, but it's important... so I do it.

Another example is from ABC's *Good Morning America* and *The View*'s Sara Haines.

She's in her dream career, but when I asked her about the "Suck Factor" of her job, she responded in a nano-second. She said, "I'm totally a sweatshirt and jeans girl. I know some people would love the fashion aspects of my job... having to wear something different every day, but I don't. That stuff just doesn't come natural to me. But I deal with it because it's a part of the job and it's so small in comparison to the things I love about what I do."

[To listen to this interview with Sara, go here: MitchMatthews.com/010.]

That's the key. The goal isn't to 100% eliminate the "Suck Factor." That's not realistic. But my goal for you (and it's my goal for me too) is to keep the "Suck Factor" to 20% or less of what you do.

Cuz hey... if you're hitting "80% LOVE," the "20% SUCK" is totally acceptable.

Plus... life is hard. It can be awesome... amazing... and incredible. But some of it is just straight up hard. If anyone tells you otherwise, they're either selling something or smoking something. :)

If we can agree on this, then we can also agree that keeping the right attitude is imperative.

> *"People often say that motivation doesn't last. Well neither does bathing -- that's why we recommend it daily."*
> - Zig Ziglar

So here are two super foods when it comes to keeping the right attitude.

Gratitude and Curiosity.

GRATITUDE:

First we'll talk about gratitude briefly.

It's a hot topic lately, and I'm glad.

> *"Develop an attitude of gratitude, and give thanks for everything that happens to you, knowing that every step forward is a step towards achieving something bigger and better than your current situation."*
> - Brian Tracy

Gratitude is your body's natural antidepressant. When you take the time to intentionally feel grateful, your body releases serotonin and dopamine. These naturally occurring chemicals have been shown to help people feel less depressed and more happy. They also help you to be more creative and feel more peaceful too. (Who doesn't want more of ALL of that?)

Craig Ballentyne spoke to this specifically in my interview with him. He's a successful entrepreneur, blogger, and fitness expert. In fact, gratitude plays a central role in his "Perfect Day Formula," which is his daily regimen for maximizing each and every day.

One of his daily rituals is to list out 3 to 5 things he feels grateful for every day. As he writes them down he takes a few moments to really feel gratitude for each item. It might be that he had a good meeting with a client, or that he shared a nice meal with a friend, or that he has a fun trip coming up, or that the weather was particularly pleasant yesterday. They don't have to be big things... elaborate things... expensive things. They can be simple. The key is to really feel a sense of gratitude as you list them out.

[To listen to this interview with Craig, go here: MitchMatthews.com/130.]

CURIOSITY:

Curiosity is the other key.

Advertising executive Sam Griffin said it best when I talked with him about how he created his dream career of traveling the world and working with top brands like Cosmopolitan, Oprah Magazine, and Volvo.

In our conversation, he threw out a phrase I loved.

It was, "The opposite of fear is curiosity."

He explained that, in the face of fear, he would intentionally push himself to be curious.

For example, when he was completing his degree at Iowa State University, he was faced with a number of career choices. One was with a company in Iowa and the second was with a solid organization in Kansas City (just 3 hours from where he grew up).

The third was to take a chance and move to New York City and try to get on with a top magazine there. All were good options, but the one that excited AND horrified him the most was taking the NYC route. He pushed through the fear by becoming curious.

Instead of focusing on the things he was afraid of, he started to ask himself questions. He stirred up his curiosity. What would it be like? Who might he meet? How could he make it work?

He moved to the Big Apple. He hustled. He stayed curious.

And as a result... he shaped a dream career.

[To listen to this interview with Sam, go here: MitchMatthews.com/118.]

So how about it?

No matter where you're at right now... can we agree to move forward with some gratitude and a little curiosity?

What might happen?

I can't wait to find out.

GRATITUDE ACTIVITY:

Let's get a little serotonin and dopamine flowing for you.

Answer the following question:

What are 3 things (big or small) you could feel grateful for... right now?

Once you've done that, take a minute to really feel the gratitude for these things. [Good job!]

CURIOSITY ACTIVITY:

Let's stir up a little curiosity too.

Where could you be using some of Sam's Curiosity Questions?

- What might I learn?
- Who might I meet?
- What are some good things that could come on the other side of _____?

Think about it and write down a few areas in your life where you want to intentionally become more curious.

NOTES:

Chapter Two

B - BRIDGE

Your next job probably won't be a Dream Job.

I'm not being a nay-sayer.

In fact, I'm being the opposite.

I'm shooting straight with you.

This is simply what I found... time and time again... in my own experience. Plus, I saw it over and over in my interviews with people who'd achieved Dream Jobs.

Before there was a Dream Job... there was almost always a "BRIDGE JOB."

So, if your next job isn't a Dream Job... let's intentionally make it a Bridge Job.

What's the difference between a Dream Job and a Bridge Job?

As we've discussed, a Dream Job allows you to do

work you love and/or it allows you to do something outside work that you love. A Dream Job feels like home. It feels like a place you want to stay. It's where you achieve "flow" a lot [Source: https://en.wikipedia.org/wiki/Flow_(psychology)].

You can lose track of time because you get so caught up in what you're doing. It's where you're challenged... but you love the challenge most days.

It's work that's the right fit for this season of your life.

That's a Dream Job.

A Bridge Job is just that... a bridge.

Think about a bridge. It's not a place you want to stay a long time. It's built to get you somewhere.

It's okay that you don't want to stay there the rest of your life. Don't!

But while you're there, maximize the opportunity.

The key is, when you're in a Bridge Job, focus on what I call the "M.E.A.L. Plan."

M.E.A.L. Plan:

○ **MEET** - Who can you meet?

○ **EARN** - What can you earn?

○ **AVAILABLE** - What can you be available to do/ try/experience?

○ **LEARN** - What can you learn?

SIDE NOTE: If you start talking about going after a Dream Job... you can say to your nervous-Nelly friends and/or parents, "Don't worry. I have a 'M.E.A.L. Plan' at my new company." They'll think you've scored a job at one of those cool Google- type organizations with an all-you-can-eat cafeteria and nap pods. Plus, they'll assume you're being very prudent and believe you're intent on feeding yourself as you pursue your dreams. Well played... well played.

The M.E.A.L. Plan...

Who can you MEET? What can you EARN? What can you be AVAILABLE to do? What can you LEARN?

Think of these four categories as a Venn Diagram.

ADDITIONAL SIDE NOTE: People who write personal development books must adhere to a code. A set of laws... enforced by a secret society based in Geneva. Part of the code is that you must include at least one Venn diagram and at least one acronym. But hey... I'm taking care of both in one chapter. Look at me go! Woot woot.

DREAM JOB: Redefined - M.E.A.L. Plan™

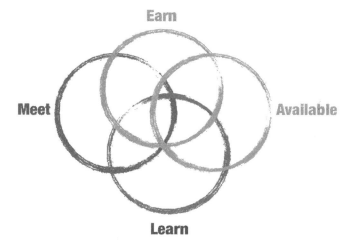

Let's break each of these down and give you real-world examples for each category.

MEET:

Award-winning reporter and journalist Antonio Neves graduated from college and moved to New York with almost no money or connections. (He had $600 to his name when he stepped off the train.) He didn't have enough experience to nail down a Dream Job. Plus, due to the high cost of living in NYC, he knew he needed to score a job... quick.

Antonio wanted to be in entertainment and news. He wasn't exactly sure what his Dream Job was when he started this process, but he was committed to figuring it out as he went.

He got strategic. He went after a Bridge Job that would allow him to MEET the right kinds of people.

The solution wasn't glamorous. In fact, it was more than a bit humbling. But this former D-1 athlete and holder of a Master's Degree from the Columbia University Graduate School of Journalism took a data-entry-level temp job. The key was that it was at VIACOM, which is the parent company to networks like Comedy Central, CMT, BET, Paramount Pictures, and Nickelodeon, to name a few.

He did a good job. He worked hard. And... on his breaks... he would reach out and meet new people.

He'd connect and invite peeps to coffee or lunch and get to know them. He'd express authentic interest in what they did and ask questions about how they got there.

Over the course of a short time, he started to have friends throughout the building. Eventually, one of those new friends asked Antonio to fill in as an extra on a show for Nickelodeon. So during his lunch hour, he slipped up to a sound studio and participated in the recording. That led to another invite, and another. Before he knew it, Antonio had secured a reoccurring role.

His relationships within the building continued to grow. Plus, he started to connect with other leaders his new network of friends introduced him to. He kept demonstrating hard work and authentic interest in others. Those conversations led Antonio to opportunities to be a correspondent and producer with other top networks including NBC, PBS, BET, and E! News.

He's now in his dream career in LA, and it started with a Bridge Job focusing on who he could MEET.

[To listen to this interview with Antonio, go here: MitchMatthews.com/004.]

EARN:

Often a Bridge Job will allow you to EARN needed funds so you can have a roof over your head and food in your fridge. You might not LOVE the work, but you can give a tip of the hat in gratitude to a job that allows you to make ends meet while still pursuing a path towards work that satisfies.

Diego Corzo is a great example of this.

When Diego graduated from Florida State University, he had his degree but he wasn't really sure what he wanted to do with his career. He wound up taking a job with GM that moved him to Austin, Texas.

He wasn't crazy about the work (he was coding and building websites), but it provided a solid income. He worked hard and delivered excellence while on the job. But in his off time, he decided to experiment and try new things.

He read books like *Rich Dad/Poor Dad* by Robert Kiyosaki. That led him to pursue a new interest in real estate. His first investment was purchasing a house of his own that had extra rooms he could rent out. Within a few months, he was covering his mortgage payment thanks to three other programers who rented his extra bedrooms.

Diego continued to be curious about other facets of real estate so he found a local realtor he could shadow. In fact, he offered to be this agent's driver and personal assistant at nights and on the weekends. In return for driving the agent around to his appointments, he agreed to answer Diego's many questions and teach him about the business.

The more he learned, the more Diego found he loved this type of work.

Boom! He'd found his dream career track.

Now, one of the things Diego learned was that it takes time to build a real estate career. So as he continued to work hard for GM during the day, he also began to build his own real estate business on the side.

I want to stress this point. Diego continued to work diligently for GM. He continued to set a high standard for himself. At the same time, he continued to work nights and weekends on the dream too.

His side business started to grow and within a few years, he was able to launch his full time career in real estate and rental investments. Now, at 26 years old, Diego is a successful realtor with Keller Williams and he owns several rental properties too.

Diego made it a point to never let his work slip at GM, even though he was pursuing his dream on the side. This paid off on multiple levels.

1.) He could look at himself in the mirror every day and know that he was giving his best work.

2.) He continued to get promoted and receive new opportunities during his time at GM.

3.) Since he didn't burn any bridges or abuse the opportunity, many of his real estate clients are now referrals from his contacts at GM.

4.) He continued to EARN a solid income that enabled him to keep a roof over his head, pay for training and needed certifications, AND purchase properties too!

[To listen to this interview with Diego, go here: MitchMatthews.com/132.]

AVAILABLE:

Some of the people who had achieved or created their Dream Jobs had chosen Bridge Jobs because of what it made them AVAILABLE to do, try, or experience.

For example, Lise Cartwright is now a full-time writer and a bestselling author of over 23 books. She lives in New Zealand, but celebrates the fact that she could run her business from anywhere in the world. In fact, that flexibility is one of the aspects of writing that makes it her current Dream Job.

She didn't always have that flexibility.

When she started to get serious about setting a new course for her life, Lise started to get intentional about her work. Her job wasn't satisfying and the more she looked down the road, she didn't like where things seemed to be heading. She had an idea of what her dream involved. She'd always loved writing. She was pretty darn good at it too. But she didn't feel like she had enough experience to make a living from it yet.

She needed a BRIDGE.

So she decided to make a change and take an administrative position. It was far from a Dream Job, but it was the type of work that allowed her to have a very predictable schedule. Plus, it was work that wouldn't follow her home. Once the day was done, she could leave her desk and not think about it again until the next day at 8 am.

This choice made her more AVAILABLE to start experimenting with writing.

First, she started to offer her services as a freelancer. At the same time, she started to write her first book. She'd leave her Bridge Job at 5 pm, come home, take a break, have some dinner and then start writing.

She'd work from 6:30 pm to 8:00 pm most nights. It was just 90 minutes. But it started to add up. She helped clients and she prepped to launch her first book. Over time, more clients came and she wrote more books too.

Eventually, the income from her freelance work and her books made it possible for Lise to leave that Bridge Job and launch into her writing career... full time. A big part of what made that possible was the availability that came from her Bridge Job.

[To listen to this interview with Lise, go here: MitchMatthews.com/015.]

LEARN:

A number of the people I interviewed told me a tough realization hit them as they started to get clear on their next Dream Job.

They began to acknowledge there were things they still needed to learn... especially when it came to making a shift and doing more of the work they were passionate about.

That was Sara Haines' case. (I mentioned Sara in the previous chapter.) Sara had graduated with a degree in political science but she wanted to pursue a career in the world of news and entertainment. Although she was excited about the possibilities, Sara knew she had a lot to learn. So she moved to the New York City area, lived on her brother's couch in Central Jersey, and took a long train ride into the city... daily.

She wanted to be in the heart of it.

She'd figured out a way to live simply... so the EARN circle wasn't top of mind. Nope. For Sara, her Bridge Job needed to be about what she could LEARN.

Through a lot of hard work she was able to score a coveted position in the NBC Page Program.

This was a less-than-glamorous intern-level position with long hours and low pay. She spent her days seating audience members for various shows, ordering catering, and making sure the right people got to the right spots at the right times. But she also took every opportunity she could to LEARN.

She spent time with anyone and everyone in order to learn the various aspects of creating a show. She talked with producers, directors, camera operators, and even branding team members. She got to know them and learned about what they did on a day-to-day basis. Plus, she also took acting and improv classes at night to develop her skills and prepare for being in front of the camera some day.

She worked hard. Day in and day out.

That led to a Production Coordinator position on the *Today Show*. Although it was closer to her dream... it was still far from a Dream Job.

At this point, NBC had just experienced cutbacks. So her new role was something that had previously been filled by two people. Plus, the *Today Show* had just been extended by an additional hour. So this new position made for some very long days, but she kept working and learning.

Then it happened.

In addition to the budget cutbacks, this was also right at a time when NBC was asking its most notable talent to try to create online content. Sara saw an opportunity to apply all that she'd been learning... and take a step closer to her dream. She was tasked with asking a few questions of a musician who had just performed a concert on the Plaza at Rockefeller Center.

Traditionally, a coordinator would do this off-camera, but Sara was hit with an idea. She quickly asked for permission to do the interview on camera with the star. The producer agreed and Sara nailed the interview. In fact, the other producers and people who saw it loved it and they told Sara she needed to brand it. So she called her friends in the graphics department (people she'd connected with, learned from, and helped in the past) and asked them to create a logo for the segment. They called it "Backstage Pass" and quickly sent her a design.

The interview was loaded on NBC's site and it was an instant hit.

That led to other opportunities which grew into Sara becoming a correspondent on the fourth hour of the *Today Show*. Next came a regular spot on ABC's *Good Morning America*. And now she's living the newest chapter of her dream career as a daily cast member on ABC's *The View*.

In our last interview, Sara expressed how grateful she was for that first Bridge Job... and how she still applies all that she learned there... daily.

[You can listen to my two interviews with Sara here: MitchMatthews.com/010 and here: MitchMatthews.com/032.]

MEAL PLAN CASE STUDY:

Now that you're getting the picture of the four elements within the M.E.A.L. Plan, I wanted to offer another example.

It's how I used the M.E.A.L. Plan to select the last Bridge Job I had before launching my own company.

At the time, I had been in the pharmaceutical industry for about five years. I had worked my way up to be a Program Training Manager for a $2 billion company. This position had been a dream for me. It allowed me to grow as a speaker and facilitator. I was also getting to do a lot of coaching, which I really enjoyed as well. Plus, I was getting to design training day in and day out.

This position had been a Dream Job, BUT things shifted in my life.

I could feel a change coming.

There was a longing.

Although I enjoyed the work in the training department, and I'd aspired to achieve this particular role... deep down inside, I wanted to be an entrepreneur. I wanted to grow a business that could have a positive and powerful impact on the world.

So although I was in a Dream Job, I recognized that I needed to start to prepare for my next Dream Job. The more I thought about it... the more I knew this transition was going to call for me to find a new Bridge Job.

Just to give some additional context, my training position had caused us to move to Chicago, which was 6 to 9 hours away from our extended families. We had two children under the age of 3 and my wife and I longed for our boys to grow up close to their grandparents.

Then... I had an experience in a Hallmark store that pushed me over the edge. It was the final straw that persuaded me it was time for a change.

It's kind of a goofy story... but at the same time it was important... so I'll share it.

I remember it vividly. I had stopped at the mall on my

way home from work to grab a birthday card for a friend. While I was standing there looking at the various options, I noticed an elderly gentleman standing two sections down from me. Then... out of the corner of my eye... I saw a big kid walk in wearing a letterman's jacket from a local high school. I guessed he was a football player because he had shoulders like Dwayne "the Rock" Johnson. His size made him stand out but his odd behavior was what really made me pay attention.

As he walked into the store, he immediately crouched down and started to sneak through the rows of cards. He was on a direct course towards me. I wasn't sure whether I should get ready for a fight or be prepared to scream like a little girl... but he quickly passed me and proceeded to grab the elderly man standing five feet away.

The young athlete enveloped his victim in a big bear hug from behind. Once he released his startled prey, the surprised gentleman spun around to address his attacker. His response surprised me even more because instead of yelling at the kid, the elderly man dropped down into a position similar to a Sumo wrestler preparing for a match. He muttered, "It's go time," as a Bruce Willis type grin came across his face. The high schooler matched the stance... and I thought there was going to be a brawl right there in the middle of the birthday card section. They held each other's gaze for a few seconds and then the young man smiled and simply said, "Grandpa!" and they gave each other another big hug.

It was at that point that it struck me.

For the next season of my life... my Dream Job would also involve being able to have my family live close to grandparents. I just knew that I wanted my boys to have the experience of being able to bump into their grandpa in a store on a random Tuesday afternoon.

So... after talking with Melissa (my wife) and giving it some more prayer and thought, I started to set a new course towards being able to bring my family back to Iowa AND to eventually start my own business.

BUT... I knew I wasn't fully ready for that.

So I needed a BRIDGE.

Here's how I used the M.E.A.L. Plan to select the right job for me in that season.

I started to think through my options.

Since I was already in a management position, I could have tried to be a field manager in Iowa with the company I was with or with a different company. But I knew that type of position would involve a lot of travel and crazy busy schedules. Although the pay would have been great, that type of role wouldn't have allowed me to be the husband and father I wanted to be. Plus, it wouldn't have helped me to grow in the ways I needed to grow in order to move towards my next Dream Job of being an entrepreneur.

So I switched companies and gave myself a bit of a demotion by leaving management and going back to a position as a pharmaceutical sales person in Iowa.

Although I didn't love the idea of going back to a role I'd felt like I'd graduated out of, when I considered the M.E.A.L. Plan, I knew it was the right decision. It got us back to Iowa so we could be close to family... and I could start to prepare for my next Dream Job.

MEET -

Unlike Antonio's story, my new job didn't mean I'd be working with the types of people that might help me to prepare for entrepreneurism in the normal course of my day. In fact, my day to day schedule meant that I'd be interacting with doctors, nurses, hospital administrators, and other sales people. So although these people were wicked smart... and many of them were pure awesome... there weren't a lot of people in this bunch that could teach me about building a business.

However, although I knew I wouldn't meet a lot of entrepreneurial-minded people during the natural course of my day, the job did allow me a more flexible schedule. Plus, I was traveling a lot. So I could make the time to meet with entrepreneurs and innovative thinkers in each of the communities I covered before and after work.

Meeting the right people... check.

EARN -

I'll admit it. When we moved back to Iowa from Chicago for this new job, we splurged a bit on our house. We'd been living in a small house in Chicago, so when we came back to our home state, we went big with our home.

We found a beautiful place on an acre of land in the country. It was really nice. But it was also pricey.

As a result, we started living what I now call the S.I.T.C.O.M. life. (Single Income Two Children Oppressive Mortgage.)

It wasn't the smartest decision we ever made... but hey, I promised I'd shoot straight with you. That's where we were.

So... the EARN category was something I had to pay attention to. This sales position certainly wasn't a Dream Job but it helped me to earn what I needed to at the time.

AVAILABLE -

Although I traveled a bit with my new role, I was always at home on Fridays. So I started to have coffee with different business people and thought leaders in my area every Friday morning at 7 am. I could do that meeting before launching into my day.

Plus, because I knew the ins-and-outs of my job and because I was really in charge of my own schedule, I could sign up for night classes and attend networking events.

I didn't love the day-to-day work of my pharmaceutical sales position, but it offered the needed flexibility so I could grow my network, my knowledge, and my experience.

LEARN -

The actual work of the job was rather mundane. I'd been a pharma salesperson for years and there wasn't a lot that was new in the job. However, my sales territory covered an entire state, so I spent a lot of time in my car. (Three hours a day... on average.)

I knew this going in and it was actually a huge selling feature of the job for me. Why? Because those hours looking through a windshield each day allowed me to earn my M.B.A. degree (Masters in Bad-Assery).

Seriously... I listened to 2000+ hours of audio books on business strategy, innovative thinking, leadership, marketing, branding, personal effectiveness, communication styles, and personality types.

And... on Fridays, I'd treat myself and listen to sci-fi and western audio novels. (Geeks gotta have a little fun too!)

So that's how the M.E.A.L. Plan helped me to select that Bridge Job.

I told myself that I might need to be in it for up to 5 years because I wasn't sure how long it would take to launch my business. But through God's grace... a lot of coffee... some good planning... and a little luck... I was able to go full-time as an entrepreneur in two years and one month. Woot woot!

Just a quick reminder here. I didn't love that work. In fact, some days were really rough.

But I was still committed to delivering excellence while I was doing it. I prided myself in serving my customers and honoring my manager. I wanted to be able to sleep well at night and know that I wasn't abusing the opportunity. Plus, I had a goal that 10 years down the road... after I'd launched my business full time and was successful... if I ran into my old boss, one of my customers, or a team member, I'd be able to look them in the eye and know that I'd delivered my best work when I worked for/with them.

That might seem weird to some, but I bet YOU get it.

EXCELLENCE -

I know I don't have to tell YOU this, but even though it's a Bridge Job... this isn't permission to slack... to slide... or to check out.

Almost everyone I interviewed had some Bridge Jobs in their journey to their current Dream Job, but all of them worked hard and brought their best to those jobs.

Bring excellence.

Do great work.

Treat people well.

The payoff? You can hold your head high. Sleep well at night. Develop relationships that will pay off down the road.

I love how NASCAR's Jon Housholder put it in an interview I did with him. We were talking about the importance of bringing your best work... even when you're in a Bridge Job... and he said,

"You'll never regret excellence."

That's true.

I'm betting you agree.

So... when thinking through your current job... or a possible new Bridge Job... consider your M.E.A.L. Plan. Think about who you can MEET, what you can EARN, what you can be AVAILABLE to do, and what you can LEARN.

You can either choose a new job or retrofit your current job to maximize your M.E.A.L. Plan.

Oh... and as you do... deliver with excellence with a big smile on your face... because you're on your way towards a career you'll love and work that matters. Plus, you'll be doing it on your terms.

Okay... so that's the Bridge Job concept.

How could YOU apply it?

Give it some thought.

Then... dive into this activity and see where it takes you.

Application of your M.E.A.L. Plan:

Okay, so now you understand the circles within the M.E.A.L. Plan and how they've worked in other people's lives.

So let's think about YOUR own M.E.A.L. Plan and how you could either find a new job or retrofit your current job based on the circles.

LET'S LOOK BACK

One of the best ways to train your brain to identify opportunities for the M.E.A.L. Plan in the present and in the future is to look at your past.

In the next activity, we're going to take a look at one to three of the jobs you've held in the past.

As you do... respond to the questions listed below.

NOTE: These could be any kinds of jobs. They could be paid, unpaid, volunteer, and/or my--parents-made-me-do-it-every-Saturday kind of jobs. Think back and describe where elements of the M.E.A.L. Plan might have existed in some small but significant way.

Previous Job: _____

What parts of M.E.A.L. existed here?

Did you MEET people who would help you in some way?

Were you able to EARN some money to pay for things you needed?

Did the job make it so you could be AVAILABLE for other things in your life at the time? (School? Kids? Projects/Hobbies/Side Hustles?)

Did the job allow you to LEARN something... either directly or indirectly?

Previous Job: _____

What parts of M.E.A.L. Plan existed here?

Previous Job: _____

What parts of M.E.A.L. Plan existed here?

Notes and observations about other jobs from your past:

LET'S LOOK FORWARD

Answer the questions below and see where they take you.

MEET:

What types of people would you like to be meeting

right now? Who would you love to be learning from?

Where are these types of people hanging out? Where are they working?

EARN:

How much would you like to be earning right now?

Are there any areas in your life where you could simplify to lower that number? (If so, where?) What might that feel like?

Are there any ways to increase what you're earning right now? (Starting a side job/side hustle? Asking for a raise? Finding a new job? Selling some things?)

AVAILABLE:

If you had a little extra time, what would you do with

it? How would you spend an extra hour or two a day if you had it?

What types of positions/jobs might allow you to have some extra time?

What things could you eliminate or reduce in your current schedule to make room for some additional time?

LEARN:

What types of things would you love to learn about?

What are some ways you could learn about them? (Take a class? Read a book? Listen to an audio book? Listen to a podcast? Ask a friend?)

What types of jobs might allow you to learn about these things?

NOTES:

Chapter Three

C - CLUES

I've been a Success Coach since 2002.

If someone asks me who my ideal coaching client is, I usually reply:

My ideal client is a fun, successful person who is on the road which brought them their success. BUT... as they look down that road... they're not sure they want to stay on it. They see some "off ramps" coming but they're not sure which one to take... or if they should take one at all. But in their heart of hearts... they want to know they're on the right road... so they can stomp on the gas and go.

Yup. That's who I do my best coaching work with.

I've had clients from all walks of life. I've worked with entrepreneurs to attorneys, marketing directors to real estate moguls, pastors to psychologists, and college professors to recent college grads.

As I've done this work... helping people figure out the

"right road" for them career-wise... I've found they all long for billboards. They want big, bold and clear signs that will point them in the right direction.

We all do, right?

A BIG sign that says:

- "This is the RIGHT career choice for you! You'll love it."
- "I know you're nervous but post for THIS job. It'll be a perfect fit!"
- "Don't take THAT job. The pay is good but you'll hate the work!"
- "When he asks... just say, "No thank you," and walk away!!!!"

Billboards.

Bold indicators that help to make things clear.
Signs that help to eliminate all doubt and risk.
Placards that tell you exactly where to go and when to go there.

That would be great. Wouldn't it?

The challenge is... those types of billboards rarely exist.

That's the bad news.

The good news is that although those clear signs rarely make an appearance in this road trip we call a career, there's something else that can help guide us.

They are more subtle.

You have to look for them.

BUT when you start to pay attention, they are everywhere!

What are they?

I call them "clues."

That's right.

You might need to channel your inner Sherlock Holmes, but as we start to help you get more clarity on what your next Dream Job might be, we're going to start looking for clues.

To locate these clues, we don't need a magnifying glass or any of the cool tools or gadgets they use on *CSI* or NCIS. Nope.

We just need questions.

I call them "Clue Questions."

- What are a few things you are naturally good at?
- What are some things you enjoy doing?
- When's the last time you got so wrapped up in a task you lost track of time? Describe it.
- What has been one of your favorite jobs/roles (paid or unpaid)? Why was it a favorite?
- What's something about your current job you really enjoy?
- What's something about your current job you would change?

These types of questions help you uncover important clues that will begin to guide you.

When I interviewed the hundreds of people in Dream Jobs, I saw "Clue Questions" pop up in their stories.

For example, when I interviewed Spencer Griffin, Executive Producer and Senior Vice President of Big Breakfast, CollegeHumor.com's production company, he talked about how these types of questions helped at a very pivotal time in his life.

He explained that after graduating from college, he went into what he called "a bit of a tailspin."

He graduated with a degree in theater but at first he worked at a bar. Then he was an assistant at Miramax Films. Next he worked in another bar, and then he traveled with a company coordinating events. After that, he lived overseas teaching English for a short time and then came to NYC in another event coordination role.

None of these positions lasted more than about 6 months.

Towards the end of this season, he really started to inventory his skills.

He started to look for clues.

He asked himself... even with his rather random job history... what had he done well? What had he enjoyed? What came naturally? He even went back to his college days to think about some of the other roles and volunteer positions he'd held.

As he did, he started to see some patterns emerge.

He started to see some clues.

For example, when he was in school, he and some friends had started an art gallery/theater above their favorite bar. They were able to sell art and put on small plays and shows. They might have violated a few fire codes along the way, but Spencer led the charge on figuring out how to make enough money to keep the doors open and even turn a profit. As he continued to think about it, he saw his biggest successes were related to working with people, organizing things, and hitting timelines.

He said, "I had to swallow my pride. I went to school for directing and playwriting. I was pretty good for high school and I was fine for a college student. But I wasn't professional playwright material." Spencer continued, "... I think people say 'follow your passions' a lot. They say 'follow your dreams.' As a thirty-something now, I get it. But as a 22-year-old, I was confused as to what my passion was. Because I had thought it was theater. But I started to realize that wasn't it. When I started to think about it... I realized I was really good at corralling creative people."

He continued, "I am the most business-minded artist I know, and I'm the most artistic business guy I know," he said, inventorying his own clues. "I had to go, 'I'm not going to be a professional playwright. Well, that's okay. I'm going to be fine.' What do I love about playwriting? It's creating stories, telling stories, and working with creative people."

He then went for a post-production coordinator position at CollegeHumor.com and even though he didn't have any experience in film, he could point to his experience at managing timelines, working with people, and getting things done. He also relayed how his "varied" work history and event experience had prepared him to work with VIPs of successful organizations and that he would be able to "learn it on the job."

They bought it.

They hired him.

He worked really really hard.

It's paid off... big time.

It didn't happen immediately, but fast forward a few years and now he's producing video projects featuring the likes of Jason Bateman, Will Arnett, Rhett & Link, Adam Conover, and others.

More importantly, he's loving his work.

Spencer said, "When you find stuff that you love, you become this better version of yourself. You work a little harder. You see a little clearer. Your work is better. To me, that matters. I'm happy at my job, and therefore I'm good at my job."

Clues.

They might not be obvious at first but keep digging.

A LIST MIGHT HELP:

As you start to think about the things you're good at... the things you enjoy... the things you lose track of time while doing... sometimes it helps to see a list of possibilities. It can prime the pump and get the juices flowing. Here's a list of roles I often show audiences and coaching clients when we're talking about looking for clues.

This isn't a comprehensive list and it's not in any particular order, but it might help to spark some ideas.

Create	Use/create Systems
Lead	Mentor
Sell	Produce
Organize	Negotiate
Teach	Travel
Design	Write
Use Technology	Use Media
Use Math	Use Science
Entertain	Connect
Have fun	Hit Timelines

Manage	Translate
Coach	Serve
Walk in Faith	Encourage
Finance	Perform
Use Data	Plan
Research	Vision
Promote	Care
Build	Deconstruct

Okay... here are a few more "Clue Questions" based on this list of potential roles.

MORE CLUE QUESTIONS:

Which of these words jump out at you?

Which of these concepts make you smile?

Which of these ideas make you cringe? (Let's stay away from those.)

Of the two to three (or more) words you connect

with... think through the following:

- Describe a time when you were able to _____ and it went well.
- What happened?
- What went well? (Celebrate the big and the small wins!)
- What did you enjoy about it?

Seriously... do this exercise a few times and just see where it takes you.

Now... don't worry.

Don't expect the clouds to part, the sun to shine and harps to spontaneously begin to play as a unicorn starts to spell out your Dream Job in puffy rainbow letters in the sky.

Nope. Don't shoot for that. (You don't need that kind of pressure!)

Just have some fun with this and see where it takes you.

We're just looking for clues right now.

Clues are important.

They add up.

And they'll help us as we move forward.

Oh, and if your "inner critic" starts to grumble in your head and ask, "Is there really a job that involves _____?"

You can say to that grumpy ol' voice... "Well, yes, there is. But I'm just looking for clues right now!" And then get back to work on journalling some responses to the specific Clue Questions in the activity at the end of this chapter.

(Note: You might not want to respond to that inner voice with your outside voice... especially if you're doing this exercise at your desk at work, while on a train, or when you're sitting at your favorite coffee shop... because people will look at you a little funny. I'm telling you this from experience.)

KEY STRATEGY: Think "ROLES" not "TITLES"

When you start to look for clues, don't try to match them up with a specific job title right away.

That's right. It's tempting, but try not to fixate on a

specific title.

Figure out what you're good at and what you want to do more.

Really try to do this independent of whether you know a specific job title exists or not.

Most people I talked with who had attained or created a Dream Job didn't know the job existed when they started to pursue it. They just knew the type of work they wanted to do and started to go after that.

For example, as Spencer began to look for clues, he started to realize that he was really good at "corralling creatives," managing timelines, and organizing things. He looked for opportunities to do those types of things more and more. He volunteered for projects. He offered to help. He even learned how to use Excel (collective gasp!). But the more he worked in those roles... the more opportunities he got. He didn't start out looking for the title that he has now, but instead, he looked for opportunities to do more of the things he was good at.

I have a mantra when I'm helping people to uncover their next Dream Job and it's especially helpful when you're working within an organization.

"Think Roles Not Titles"

For example, if you've looked around the company you're currently in and you've seen some jobs that really interest you... great. Try not to fixate on the title.

Instead, ask yourself:

- What interests you about that position?
- What types of things might you get to do if you achieved that title?
- What excites you about that position?

There are three main reasons I bring this up.

1.) Titles change all the time.

When they do, it can be pretty darn discouraging to a person who's really had their heart set on it. BUT... if you've thought through the roles associated with that position, you might be able to find other positions that would offer you the opportunity to play out those roles in different ways.

2.) If you lock into a particular title, it's very easy to start to feel stuck.

Unless your company is growing really quickly and/or experiencing a lot of change, it can take some time before a particular position opens up. But if you're able to identify the types of roles you want, you might be able to find other positions that would allow you to bring *your awesome*... in similar but different ways.

3.) As you start to identify the roles that interest you most...

You can also start to identify areas where you want and need to continue to develop. Since you're focused on the role instead of the title, you're going to be more open. If you're fixated on one particular title, you might be blinded to opportunities that come available, since they're not always associated with that position.

For example, I was recently working with a tech firm on this concept. I was talking with someone who was in quality assurance. As he started to look for "clues" to figure out where he might want to go next, he started to realize he was really good at leading special project teams. Although he didn't have any positional authority in these situations, he still helped progress happen across departments.

Up to this point, he had really been thinking his next move was a particular position in his department that would allow him to use more of his technical skills but wouldn't involve much leadership. So he held loosely to the title and started to focus on the roles that interested him the most. As a result, he started to sign up for mentoring classes, communication strategy workshops, and generational leadership courses. These were all things that hadn't been on his radar before, but since he was looking at his career path from a "roles" perspective, it started to open up new possibilities. Within a year, he had moved into a new leadership position. When he got it, he was prepared, and it fit like a glove.

So... "Think Roles Not Titles" and go after these Clue Questions:

PAST:

When have you felt successful? Think of three specific times. What were you doing? Describe the situation. What "roles" were involved?

PRESENT:

What are two to three things you enjoy about your current work?

What would you like to do more?

What would you like to do less?

What types of opportunities just seem to be coming to you?

What types of opportunities do you enjoy the most?

What types of roles cause you to experience flow? (That feeling where time just melts away and you get lost in your work.)

What are some things that have come naturally to you?

FUTURE:

If you were able to take on any type of role... what types of things would you do?

If money wasn't an issue... what types of things would you do with your time?

A BONUS CLUE STRATEGY:

I hope you've been able to identify a few things from the list that you love to do. Things that you're good at. Things that come naturally for you. Things you enjoy doing.

If so... pure awesome.

But... at the same time... you might be drawing a blank on jobs that involve that role. If so... here's a super simple strategy that will provide some ideas, encouragement and a bit of a boost.

Simply Google "Jobs that involve _____" and insert your word(s).

Yup. That's it.

Just try it.

In some cases, it will point you to well-known jobs utilizing those roles. In other cases, you'll find out about jobs you didn't even know existed. It can be really eye-opening! Now, again, I don't offer this strategy so that you'll fixate on a particular title... but I do suggest giving it a try to get a burst of ideas and inspiration.

NOTES:

Chapter Four

D - DREAM

Now that we've been doing some thinking about your career... it's time to open things up.

I want to take an intentional moment and give your heart and mind permission to dream.

We're not going to limit this dreaming to just your work and career.

We're going bigger.

We're going to dream about your LIFE.

All of it.

Because as we put together a dream career... it's not just about the work.

It's also about how you choose to live your LIFE.

> *"You only live once, but if you do it right, once is enough!"*
> - Mae West

It's important to dream.

We all know that.

But we rarely give ourselves the chance to do it.

Studies have shown that people who write down their dreams and goals have a much better chance of achieving them. In fact, one study by psychology professor Dr. Gail Matthews found people had a 50% greater chance of achieving their goals if they put pen to paper, over those who didn't write down their goals. (Plus, people were even more likely to succeed if they shared updates about their dream journey with a friend.)

Here's a three step process for achieving dreams:

STEP 1: WRITE DREAMS DOWN.
STEP 2: DON'T GO IT ALONE.
STEP 3: REPEAT.

Science backs this up.

The 100s of interviews I've done backs this up.

But... there's one additional body of evidence that helps to make this point too.

THE BIG DREAM GATHERING

For some additional proof of this three step approach, I point to the countless stories coming from something we do called "The BIG Dream Gathering."

These are very special events we hold around the country.

I'm a little biased... but these Gatherings are a little taste of heaven.

The events consist of people giving themselves permission to dream and then helping each other.

I kick things off with sharing about how the the BIG Dream Gathering got started. Plus, I share some fun stories of real people writing down their dreams and working to achieve them.

Then we cut everyone loose to think about their dreams, write them down on "dream sheets" and then post them on the walls.

Some people know exactly what they're going to write down before they even come in the door.

But others need some time to think about their dreams and look at other people's dreams too!

The walls start to fill up with dreams.

When that starts to happen, you can feel the possibility in the room.

Then we ask everyone to go around and offer some

encouragement to their fellow big dreamers... by leaving notes of inspiration, ideas, and offers to help.

Sometimes the notes are simple. Other times they offer specific ideas, suggestions for resources and offers to make connections or pitch in to help.

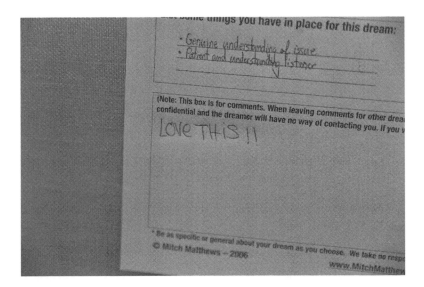

We've had all sorts of amazing stories come out of these Gatherings.

Stories of real people writing down their dreams, and then giving help and getting help.

Chandler was a junior in college when he decided to write a book after attending a BIG Dream Gathering in Chicago. He self-published and it became a bestseller. (Since then he's written 4 more bestsellers... and more are coming!)

To hear Chandler's story, listen to this interview: http://mitchmatthews.com/006

Laura was an elementary teacher who got hit with the idea of sending school supplies to Africa while attending a BIG Dream Gathering. Thanks to some encouragement, connections and help, she was able to hand deliver a shipment of globes, pencils, erasers and books to kids on the other side of the planet.

Elizabeth was a recent college graduate who posted a dream about visiting 7 continents within 10 years. At last report, she'd been able to visit 6 and is working on her remaining trip to Antartica.

Calvin wrote down several dreams at BDGs over the years. One was to simply push himself and pursue bigger dreams. That led to him achieving a dream of climbing 75 mountain summits in 75 days.

To hear Calvin's story, listen to this interview: http:// mitchmatthews.com/093

Megan was a shy junior at Drake University. She posted one dream about getting an internship and another about international travel. Someone suggested she combine the two. Megan did and spent the following summer in Berlin with a paid internship.

Mike was afraid of heights but he posted a dream about skydiving. Three weeks later he got an offer from Groupon so he went for it. He not only survived the experience but LOVED it. (NOTE: We're not sure Groupon is the best way to pick a skydiving company... but well done, MIKE!!!)

To hear more of this story, listen to this interview:
http://mitchmatthews.com/073

Mia was 9 years old when she attended her first BIG Dream Gathering. While she was there, she posted a dream about writing a book. Afterwards, her mom let me know the encouragement on her dream sheet prompted her to not wait. So that summer, she wrote a book about overcoming gossip. With some help she was able to get it into every elementary school library in her state.

You get the picture.

We've been hosting these Gatherings since 2006. So I can say without a shadow of a doubt that there is power in writing down your dreams and sharing them with a few encouraging people.

*[NOTE: I'd LOVE for you to join us. You can check out our schedule at: **www.BIGDreamGathering.com**.]*

I mention the BIG Dream Gathering and share these stories for a few reasons...

1. I hope it inspires you as you hear about other people who gave themselves permission to dream.
2. I hope it helps you give yourself permission to dream too.

It's important.

So we're going to do it.

We're going to take the critical (and fun) step of doing some dreaming.

But before we do... I want to share a strategy with you.

It might help... especially if there is a part of you that gets a little nervous at the thought of writing down some goals.

It happens. I see it every time we hold a BDG. Some people just start to lock up as they put pen to paper. Sometimes it's because they can't remember any of their dreams. But other times it's because their "inner critic" starts to hit them with questions like...

- Is that realistic?
- How could you do that?
- Is that something you REALLY want to do?
- What if it doesn't work out?
- Do you really have the money for that?
- Is that practical?
- When would I have time to do something like THAT?

Do any of these sound familiar?

If not... congratulations. You are in the 2% of people who don't worry about such things. Good for you.

But if it is something you can relate to... stay with me because I have a phrase that might help.

WILLING SUSPENSION OF DISBELIEF

This is a concept Hollywood relies on.

A "Willing Suspension of Disbelief" is critical for us as we walk through the doors of our local movie theater to watch the latest blockbuster action flick or rom-com. The term "Willing Suspension of Disbelief" has been defined as a willingness to withhold judgement and suspend critical thought for the sake of enjoyment.

Although directors like Steven Spielberg and James Cameron depend on it daily, the phrase is credited to poet and philosopher Samuel Taylor Coleridge back in 1817 when he was speaking about how powerful writing can allow someone to escape certain realities for a short period in order to enjoy a work of fiction.

Willing Suspension of Disbelief is what allows us to enjoy seeing Robert Downy Jr. build an Ironman suit in his basement overnight and fly it around the world in the morning... when our critical brain would know a team of M.I.T. scientists couldn't do THAT in 10 years.

It's what allows us to believe the beautiful couple in the latest rom-com can look amazing... 24/7... even when we ALL know NO ONE looks THAT good when they wake up!

We do it because it allows us to escape some of the harsh realities of the now. But as Coleridge explained, this willingness to suspend disbelief isn't unhealthy. In fact, this process allows us to engage our mind in thoughts, ideas, art, and theories that help us to see the world differently.

And... I believe... these short mental vacations also help us let go of some of our current limitations to be more creative, innovative and alive.

"Willing Suspension of Disbelief"

Remember that phrase as you start to dream. Then when that inner critic starts to pick at the ideas that begin to come to mind... you can shut that voice down. When you do... you aren't being crazy. You're not being irresponsible. You're not being impractical.

You're simply giving yourself an opportunity to dream without limitations.

You can tell that inner critic, "Don't worry. I'm not going to act on every one of these dreams right away."

You can even say, "Don't worry. This isn't the time to

plan. That comes later."

[Seriously... planning is in an upcoming chapter. We've got you covered!]

This is the time to dream!

Let me offer one last story to help hit this point home.

I was working with one of my success coaching clients and taking him through a similar process where he was giving himself permission to write down some of his life goals and dreams. Before we got started, I brought up the concept of "Willing Suspension of Disbelief" and reinforced the point that this wasn't a time for planning.

I said, "If a dream or goal comes to mind, don't filter it. No matter how big or impractical it might seem... don't limit yourself. Don't try to plan it. Just write it down. We'll plan later. Just dream."

I.D.K.

I went a step further and said, if his mind started to race about how he might accomplish any of the things he wrote down, then I told him to write "I.D.K."

next to that item. That stood for "I Don't Know," and it was to help him remember that now's the time for dreaming and that it was totally fine to not know the plans yet.

It was simply a healthy dose of "Willing Suspension of Disbelief."

He took me up on the exercise and brought me back a list the following week. As we looked at it together, I was blown away. There were some big dreams and some simple dreams and everything in between. There were also a number of "I.D.K.s" next to certain items.

I was proud of him. This kind of list took guts. I told him so.

Then I asked, "Was there anything on the list you were tempted to erase or take off because it just seemed too crazy or impractical?"

He paused and looked at the list again. Then a smile broke out across his face. He pointed at one item.

It was, "Own a second home in the Northwest."

He said, "I've thought about that kind of thing before but I've never allowed myself to write it down. Plus, it really doesn't make sense for where I'm at right now." And it was true. Trying to buy a second home wouldn't have been wise for him at that point in his life. His business was in flux. His son was getting ready for college. He wasn't sure he wanted to stay in his current job. BUT... it was still good to put it on the list as a dream.

I reinforced that I was proud of him and excited that he pushed through the mental filtering and wrote it down anyway. Plus, I added, "When we start to work on plans for some of these dreams... we can keep it on your radar and see where it might fit in over the next 5 to 10 years."

Later we worked together to build a five year strategy that he loved. He got back on track with his work. He shifted some things so he could do more of the things he enjoyed about his business and delegated a few things he didn't. His company started to grow and he kept walking out his plan.

We stayed in touch, but then a few years later he sent me an email.

At first I thought it was spam because the subject line read: "Check this out," and there was simply a link in the email. I replied saying, "Hey brutha. I think you got hacked. I received this weird email from you. Just wanted you to know!" He responded in a nanosecond and said, "NO! It's me. Check out the link. You're going to love it. It's my new place in Oregon!"

I clicked the link and it took me to a real estate site that showed multiple photos of a condo right on the ocean. I scrolled through the pictures and a big smile came over my face as I remembered talking through this dream with him. I quickly got him on the phone and asked for the story.

He said, "Listen. Things with the business have been going really well. But more so... ever since we talked about this dream... I've just had it on my mind. I started to talk with people about it. I took a few trips out there for business and stayed an extra day each time to poke around. I kept getting ideas. Then I was able to find this place through a friend. Believe it or not, I got a really great deal. But more importantly, it's in a little resort town. I just bought it, but I have it rented out for the next six months. I was worried that it was going to be something I couldn't afford, but the more I dug in... I realized if I did it right, I might actually make money with it. As it turns out, it's completely paying for itself already! Heck, I might even make a little money on it!"

I was blown away.

He continued, "I'm so glad I didn't filter out that dream!"

Then he yelled, "WILLING SUSPENSION OF DISBELIEF!" into the phone as if it was a battle cry!

I loved it.

So... you just never know.

How about you?

What if you gave yourself permission to dream?

What if you allowed a little willing suspension of disbelief?

What if you quieted that inner critic with a little "I.D.K." and remembered that we'll plan later?

Now's the time for dreaming.

DREAM QUESTIONS:

[You don't need to answer these in order. Scan the questions and answer the ones that interest you first. Then come back and answer the others as you go.]

What are some things you'd like to do and/or experience?

Where would you love to travel?

What types of relationships would you like to have in your life?

Who would you like to meet?

What dreams do you have for your health and fitness?

What are some of your dreams/goals for your career?

What were some of your dreams when you were a kid? Which might still apply now?

What are a few things you would like to achieve in your life?

What are some of your dreams for your family?

What are some of your dreams for your education?

What are some of your financial goals?

What are some things you would like to own someday?

Where would you love to be able to serve?

What are some of your dreams for your spiritual life?

NOTES:

Chapter Five

E - EXPERIMENT

Great job. You wrote down some of your dreams. That takes guts. Well done!

Once people give themselves permission to dream... it's exciting.

But there's something I've learned from helping thousands of people write down their dreams and goals. It's that once you've got some down on paper... it's pretty easy to get locked up.

You feel stuck.

It can happen for a number of reasons. Maybe only a few dreams came to mind and you wonder if you did something wrong. Some people worry about whether they're dreaming big enough, while others start to doubt because they think they might be dreaming too big. Then there are others still who get bogged down because they're not sure what their next step should be.

To all of this... I say, "EXPERIMENT!"

There is something very freeing about giving yourself permission to experiment.

> *"All of life is an experiment. The more experiments you make, the better."*
> - Ralph Waldo Emerson

Think about it. What if you gave yourself permission to experiment?

> *"I can never stand still.
> I must explore, and I must experiment."*
> - Walt Disney

What if you allowed yourself the opportunity try some things? You don't have to quit your job to experience something new.

You don't have to make major shifts in your life right away.

Simply experiment.

I'm not talking about crazy, wild, or even expensive experiments.

I'm talking about small but significant steps towards something new.

What if you allowed yourself to experiment... not because it would immediately lead to a new job or career... but just to find something out about yourself?

"Practice any art, however well or badly, not to get money and fame, but to find out what's inside you."
- Kurt Vonnegut

You just created a list of dreams.

Some people might consider this a "Bucket List."

You might be familiar with the concept of a "Bucket List." The basic premise has been around for a long time, but it was made more popular by a movie by the same name starring Morgan Freeman and Jack Nicholson.

The idea is you create a list of things you want to do, achieve, and/or experience before you... well... kick the bucket.

That's right.

It's the stuff you want to accomplish before you die.

People tend to put big items on their "Bucket List." Visit the Great Wall in China. Skydive. Study cooking for a week in Italy. Drive a '65 Shelby Mustang over 100 mph. Get an MBA. Meet the President of the United States.

This is great.

Hey... you know I'm the first one to say... dream big!

The challenge with the "Bucket List" is that it tends to have the same effect that I referenced before. Since the items on this list tend to be bigger... more expensive... more complicated... more involved... more time-consuming... they tend to shut a lot of people down.

The dreamer gets excited initially... but then there is a real temptation to set the list aside because they don't have the time, money or resources to make it happen.

Well... that's where I have a different strategy to offer.

It's something I call the "Experiment List."

The Experiment List

The Experiment List works right alongside your list of dreams and/or your "Bucket List."

But it's filled with smaller... more attainable... "experiments."

Things you can do right now.

You don't have to wait. You don't have to feel stuck.

You can start... in some small but significant way... today.

Let me show you how it works.

I'll apply the "Experiment List" approach to one of my own bigger dreams.

BUCKET LIST: A WEEK OF COOKING CLASSES IN FRANCE
EXPERIMENT LIST: COOKING CLASS AT A LOCAL FRENCH RESTAURANT

For example, my wife and I would love to travel to

France and/or Italy and take a cooking class for a week. To be perfectly honest, my wife would love to do the cooking classes. She's amazing in the kitchen and she loves French and Italian cuisine, so she'd love to learn from the best... in their home countries.

For me... I just like hanging out with my wife... and I like to travel... and I like to eat. So, boom... we have our big dream of traveling internationally to do some cooking. Fun stuff. Big stuff.

Admittedly, this dream also is a more significant investment of time and money. Due to busy schedules and paying for college, it's not something we can just decide to do on a whim.

But that's okay, because it's a big dream and big dreams take effort.

On the other hand, this is EXACTLY where the "Experiment List" can come in.

The Experiment List allows you to ask the question, "What's something small but significant I can do to *experiment* with this dream/goal?"

When I asked myself this question in regards to our international cooking dream, I got hit with an idea. Although we can't hop on a plane next Tuesday to jet to Paris... there is a local French restaurant that opens its kitchen once a week for a two-hour cooking class.

For a nominal fee you can spend a little time with one of their chefs watching them prepare one of the week's specials. Pretty cool.

There's also a culinary arts night class offered at our local community college.

Granted, neither offer views of the Eiffel Tower or rolling Italian hills... but they're a step. They offer an experience. They allow us to learn. They help us take some small but significant steps towards our bigger dream... together.

All for a fraction of the cost... and a fraction of the time.

Lots of learning. Low risk.

BUCKET LIST: ATTENDING THE KENTUCKY DERBY
EXPERIMENT LIST: SPENDING TIME WITH HORSES LOCALLY

Here's another fun example.

I recently had one of my success coaching clients create a list of dreams and goals. One of her items was attending the Kentucky Derby, the world famous horse race held annually in Louisville, Kentucky. Fun stuff.

She'd always watched the event with her parents when she was a child. She loved the big hats, the traditions and the excitement of what's known as the "Fastest Two Minutes in Sports."

She now had a growing family and a growing business. Her schedule was full. Plus, she and her husband had multiple small children... so her current vacation time was dominated by more family-friendly activities.

As a result, a trip to Churchill Downs was not in her immediate future.

But... we applied the "Experiment List" approach to this dream. I asked her, "What are some small but significant steps you could take towards this dream?" I added, "Heck, how could you have a little fun with it too?" I thought she might come up with trying out some large hats at a local department store... or perfecting her own recipe for a Mint Julep. (The famous drink that's a staple of the Derby.)

Access the recipe here: http://www.foodnetwork.com/recipes/alton-brown/mint-julep-recipe-1945324.

She thought about it for a minute. Then she said, "I think one of the things that fascinates me most about the race are the horses themselves. I grew up more of a city girl and I've not really had much experience with horses, but I've always wanted to ride one."

Just as I was starting to get a little concerned that she might be hatching another BIG dream of owning a horse, she stopped short and continued, "So I think I'd like to take a few riding lessons. That would be fun. Plus, there's an equestrian center just outside my town. They offer lessons for adults as well as kids. Maybe I'll take one of my daughters with me and we can experiment with it together."

Fun stuff.

Small steps. Life lessons.

BUCKET LIST: PHOTO SAFARI IN AFRICA
EXPERIMENT LIST: LEARNING ABOUT YOUR CAMERA FROM A NEIGHBOR

We had a BIG Dream Gathering participant dream of doing a photo safari in Africa. She loved watching documentaries about animals and she'd always dreamed of seeing lions, rhinos, and elephants in their natural habitat. She was dreaming big, so her goal was to spend at least three weeks traveling and exploring. As a result, she knew she needed to save up money and vacation time for a trip like this. She was excited to do it, but she also recognized that it was a few years off.

We had a chance to connect and talk about the dream. I asked some "Experiment List" questions like, "What's something small you could do now to get prepared?" I added, "What could you do that would allow you to learn something that might help you with a dream like this?"

She joked, "Well, I have a nice camera but I've never really learned how to use it. It's supposed to take great pictures but it's also pretty complicated. Even though I know it would be perfect for a trip like that, I barely know how to turn it on."

I said, "Great. How could you experiment with it?"

She thought for a moment and then responded, "I have a neighbor who loves photography. He travels all over taking pictures and he's really good. Maybe I could ask him for a little tutoring."

I said, "I love that." I continued, "I bet he'd take it as a compliment if you asked for his advice."

She agreed and said she'd ask.

She let me know the next day she gave herself permission to march across the street and talk to her neighbor and his wife. She shared a little about her dream, and let them know she really wanted to learn about photography. Then she asked if they would come over to dinner some night. In return for a nice meal, she asked for an hour of instruction. The neighbors loved the idea and took her up on the offer. Within a few hours of help, she was getting more and more confident with her camera... plus... she developed a better relationship with her neighbors too!

Experimenting.

You're getting it.

Small steps. Low cost. Low risk. Stuff you can do right now.

"What does this have to do with Dream Jobs?"

You might be thinking that the "Experiment List" totally applies to traveling the globe, skydiving, or learning how to prepare the perfect crepe... but you might be wondering how it applies to Dream Jobs and careers.

Good question.

In short. When it comes to finding or achieving Dream Jobs... experimenting is critical.

ENTREPRENUERSHIP:

One of your big dreams might be to find a career that you love. It might be to switch industries and try something totally new. Or... it might be to go for a big promotion or to start your own business.

No matter what your career-related goals and dreams are... experimenting can help get you there.

For example, when I was in the pharmaceutical sales world, I knew I wanted to start moving towards running my own business. But as I told you, we were in a financial situation that didn't just allow me to throw caution to the wind, quit my job, and try something new. I had to stay with my job... and I wanted to deliver excellence as I did.

BUT I still wanted to experiment. No, better said... I NEEDED to experiment.

The whole idea of being a life coach or a business

coach intrigued me, but I wasn't sure what it would take or how it would work. I started to experiment by first giving myself blocks of time to do research on the topic. Who was doing it? What did it look like? How had they gotten prepared to do it? Was it fun? Was it satisfying?

As I dug in, I realized that many of the most successful coaches I found had taken specific training of some kind. So I started to look for what that might look like for me. As a result, I took a three-day course on effective life coaching strategies. I didn't quit my job. I just took a long weekend to attend the class.

I gave myself permission to experiment.

As it turned out, the more I experimented... the more I realized I loved it. It lit me up. It fueled my passion for helping people. And I figured out it came pretty naturally to me. So I kept experimenting. Again, I didn't quit my job... although I wanted to. I just kept trying new things. I offered to take on a few friends as coaching clients. I took a night class on design and figured out how to create a brochure. I shared with a few people that I was coaching during the evenings and on the weekends. A friend from college referred his brother-in-law and I got my first paying client. It didn't go great. But my second paying client did.

I kept experimenting.

About two years later... all of those experiments lined up so I could finally quit my "bad fit" job and launch my full-time coaching and speaking business. It was possible thanks to the power of experimenting.

LEADERSHIP:

Maybe you're not interested in starting your own business. For you... you love the idea of leading people, but you haven't had the chance to do it. That's okay!

Find ways to experiment.

I once had a coaching client who really wanted to move into management within his organization. He was wildly talented but he was younger and new, so people didn't see him as a leader right away. As we talked about his passion for making an impact and for helping people to become better versions of themselves, we talked about ways to experiment. As a result, he volunteered for special teams. He tried not to be overzealous, but he would offer to lead projects whenever possible.

We also talked about the power of asking questions

and helping people arrive at their own solutions. He applied this by engaging with people when they seemed to be stuck. Since he was younger than most people on his immediate team, he didn't overtly offer to mentor anyone, because he wasn't sure how that would be taken. But he did look for opportunities to ask questions and help team members find new ideas. He intentionally did each of these things... volunteering... leading projects... mentoring and asking questions... as mini-leadership-experiments.

As he took this approach, he was building up valuable experience as well as growing in his influence and developing strong relationships. Within two years, he was given his first promotion into management.

SIDE NOTE: We had a follow up discussion after he'd been in his managerial role for about six months. He was quick to admit that although he'd wanted to be a manager from day one with the organization, upon reflection... he was very grateful for the two years of experimenting. He said that time was invaluable because it helped him learn more of the strategies he actually needed to lead, and it allowed him to learn them in a less stressful environment.

NON-PROFIT:

Maybe you have a goal of starting a non-profit. Great! Experiments can be a great way to get rolling in this world too!

Take Jon Vroman and his "Front Row Foundation" as an example.

Jon has always had a bent towards helping people. But after a particularly challenging situation with a friend, Jon realized there needed to be a way to bring some joy to those who are facing life-threatening diseases. While he was out on a jog with a buddy, they thought about how cool it would be to offer people who were dealing with life-threatening health issues a once in a lifetime experience... a "Front Row" experience.

They dreamed of getting them to the front row of a concert of their favorite band... or the front row of their favorite NASCAR track... or the front row of the red carpet as their favorite star passed by.

With that... the seed for the "Front Row Foundation" started to grow... experiment by experiment. They didn't have it all figured out. They just decided to try out the idea with one person in need. They found their person. They asked about her dreams. They got her and her family a limo. They got them back stage. They got her front row tickets.

As you can imagine... it was a priceless gift.

They kept experimenting. They kept growing. Learning as they went.

One experiment... and one front row experience at a time.

[You can listen to my interview with Jon here: MitchMatthews.com/034.]

[You can find out more about the Front Row Foundation here: www.FrontRowFoundation.org.]

EXPERIMENTING TO CREATE YOUR DREAM JOB

Lindsay Palmer is on my team and she's now the Event Director for the BIG Dream Gathering.

In many ways... her experiments created this job.

Let me explain.

While Lindsay was going into her senior year at

Duquesne University, she saw me speak at a summer leadership conference. I had facilitated a BIG Dream Gathering on the opening night of the conference, and then I'd taught a session on Dream Jobs the next day. She really connected with the BDG and all of the concepts focusing on finding work you love to do. In fact, I had used an example of someone who wanted to become an event planner during my talk and that lit her up. As a result, she approached me at the conference and asked if I would be open to speaking at her school if she organized the event. I agreed to explore the idea and see if we could make it work.

Lindsay returned to her campus and began to pull the event together. Lo and behold, I was speaking to a packed house at Duquesne just a few months later.

She had really impressed me with her hard work and her follow through. But she impressed me even more with the offer that came following the event.

I'd talked about the power of experimenting during my presentation and afterwards Lindsay approached me and said, "I have an experiment for you. I think I want to be an event planner but I need to get a lot more experience with it. What if we did an experiment? I know a lot of students at other colleges and universities. What if I started to reach out to them for you and promoted you to other schools? If the schools hired you, then I could help organize the events and you could pay me a percentage of your speaking fee. But I'd only get paid if you got paid. What do you think?"

It was an experiment.

It didn't cost her anything other than some time and effort.

It didn't really cost me anything other than some coaching and mentoring time.

So I agreed.

Lindsay went after it. She immediately got me booked at several schools. The experiment worked.

When she graduated, I wasn't ready to bring her on full-time. Plus, she wanted to go and have other experiences in different industries. But she kept working for me, continuing to reach out to colleges and universities at night and on the weekends. We kept experimenting with different strategies. We kept improving our systems. All while I continued to grow other aspects of my business and she continued to work a full-time job.

But things continued to click. My speaking business

exploded. The BIG Dream Gathering kept growing. And in late 2016, I was able to bring Lindsay on full time to a job that she had basically created via some hard work and a lot of experimenting.

[You can listen to my interview with Lindsay here: www.MitchMatthews.com/111.]

HOW ABOUT YOU?

What are some of your big dreams?

What's on your "Bucket List?"

From there... what are some "experiments" you could do to move you closer to some of those big dreams?

You don't have to quit school.

You don't have to quit your job. (Not right away... at least.)

Just ask yourself... what's something small... but significant... you could try?

What are some things you could do to learn more about your dream?

What are some little things that could do to prepare

for your goal... right now?

QUICK TIP:

I'm a to-do list person.

I love them. They keep my brain in check.

Lists give me small wins throughout the day.

(In fact, I'll be the first one to admit that if I do something that's not on my to-do list... I write it down... JUST SO I CAN CHECK IT OFF!!! I'm so weird. Do you do that too?)

When it comes to the topic of EXPERIMENTING... I have a special to-do list.

I call it my "15 Minute Experiment" list.

It's filled with 15-minute experiments I can do throughout my day.

When I'm waiting in line. When I'm waiting for a meeting to start. When I have a slow internet and I'm waiting for Netflix to buffer.

You get the picture.

Listen. We're all busy.

But we all tend to have 15 minute windows just pop up in our lives.

Plus, if you put them to good use... that time can really add up!

For example, if you put 15 minutes a day (five days a week) towards a dream for one year, you'll wind up with 3,900 minutes to spend over that 12 months.

That's 65 hours per year!

That math don't lie.

15 Minute Experiments

These are smaller tasks related to your bigger dreams.

They are mini-tasks that will take 15 minutes or less.

They help you to break down a big dream and continue to make progress one small step at a time.

BUT... they don't take up loads of time or money.

For example... if I'm focusing on a travel dream, I

might have some 15 minute experiments.

(As I'm writing this book, we're gearing up for a vacation to Montana. So here are some items from my current list.)

- Research hiking trails outside Bozeman, MT
- Research best restaurants in Bozeman, MT
- Research best summer sleeping bags
- Sign up for an orienteering class at my local REI Store

If I'm working on a writing a book (like I am as I write this one)... I'll have 15 minute experiments associated with it.

(Again, here are some examples from my current list.)

- Google great quotes about being intentional
- Block out a three-hour writing block next week (do this twice)
- Look at the top 50 best selling books on Amazon and take notes on covers that grab my eye

If you're working on a big dream of starting a business... you might have some items like:

- Explore LinkedIn and find people doing

something similar in your area
- Ask someone to coffee who's run their own business (sending the invitation is the 15 minute task)
- Prep 3 questions I'd like to ask an entrepreneur
- Go to iTunes and search "Lean Start Up" in the podcast -- make a note of 3 podcast episodes to listen to

If you're gearing up for a job interview... you might have some items like:

- Explore LinkedIn and find people doing something similar in your area
- Go to iTunes and search "prepping for an interview" in the podcast section -- make a note of 3 podcast episodes to listen to
- Schedule time in your calendar to listen to the podcast episodes you found

You get the picture.

Often times... the bigger the dream... the more it can overwhelm us. So we get locked up.

Creating a 15-Minute Experiment List helps you divide up the tasks needed into bite size chunks and go after them one by one. It takes the pressure off, helps you get unstuck... and it can be more fun too!

So... what are some things you're going to put on **YOUR** 15-Minute Experiment List?

NOTES:

Chapter Six

F - FAIL

It might sound counterintuitive to a successful person, but as you assemble your dream career... you have to be willing to fail from time to time.

> *"Success is not final. Failure is not fatal:*
> *It is the courage to continue that counts."*
> - Winston Churchill

Growth is the name of the game and the quest for perfection is the enemy of growth.

So... first I want to speak to the topic of "perfectionism."

I'll start by admitting:

I... Mitch Matthews... am a "recovering perfectionist."

How about you? Can you identify? Maybe you can. Maybe you know that you deal with perfectionism. If so... hang with me.

But maybe you're not sure.

Maybe you don't know that perfectionism is shutting you down.

Locking you up.

Perfectionist tendencies are often "mis-diagnosed."

Why?

Well... because many people assume that perfectionists have dustless, impeccably decorated, and well-organized homes. Living rooms that could be featured on the cover of Elle Decor. Expertly ordered and impeccably designed kitchens that would be used by the top Cooking Channel chef. Or... superbly organized and faultlessly straightened desks with every file accounted for and every pen and pencil in its designated place.

But that's not what perfectionism typically looks like.

That's not how it works.

See... perfectionists tend to be "pile people."

We don't set out to be pile people, but we are.

We come back from a meeting or a class with a handout or some notes. We hurriedly return to our desk, but since we don't have the PERFECT place to file those sheets of paper, we lay them on the corner, telling ourselves... "I'm going to file that in a bit. Especially when I find the perfect place to put it." But then a few hours or days pass and we arrive back at our desk with a packet from our most recent meeting.

We quickly place that on top of those other notes, saying to ourselves, "I'm so going to organize that later this week." A few more days pass and the pile grows. Then we find out someone important is headed our way, so we slip that unsightly pile under our desk, in a drawer, or in a box... thinking, "I'll take care of this soon... but for now... I want this place looking good!"

Yup... pile people.

Can you identify?

Also, a lot of people who deal with perfectionism are mis-diagnosed as procrastinators. Why? Well, perfectionists tend to be great starters. We love to get rocking and rolling with a project, but then when we hit about 85% to 90% we start to get locked up.

That last 10 to 15% kills us because it's not perfect. That's why we have been famous for turning in a paper at 11:59 pm if it was due at midnight. That's why we're cramming to complete that PowerPoint hours (or minutes) before the presentation.

The deadline forces us to say, "It's not perfect... but it has to be done." And we squeak through at the last minute... because the pressure of the ticking clock pushes us to deliver.

Sound familiar?

Have you felt it?

Maybe you've seen it in yourself. Maybe you've seen it in others.

Candidly... as I write this chapter... I'm sitting at my desk. As I glance to my left... I'm looking at my most recent pile... sitting on the corner of my desk right now. AND, I'll also admit, I have an impressive stack in a small box under my desk too.

Plus, it's REALLY early in the morning and I'm jamming to get things done because my deadline is early next week and it's absolutely pushing me to tell myself, "B+ is a passing grade. It doesn't have to be an PERFECT. Let's get this done!"

Hey... I said I'm a "Recovering Perfectionist."

I haven't got it completely beat but I'm better today than I was yesterday.

I bring all of this up because I believe perfectionism... and the quest for not making a mistake... not failing in some way... stops more people from creating and/or finding Dream Jobs than anything else.

I'll offer a fun story as a two-part example.

EXAMPLE... part 1.
A while back... I was flying to speak at a leadership conference for college students in New York. I was connecting through the Chicago O'Hare Airport. As I got to my connecting flight's gate they announced it was going to be delayed. So I sat down at a nearby community table to get some work done. The gate was packed, and I wound up sharing the table with a few other people. I could tell the two young men sitting across from me were college students, so I asked if they were attending the conference I was headed to. They were. So we started to talk.

One was named J.T. and the other was named Cliff.

One was reading a book about interviewing for jobs, so I asked if he was a senior. His name was Cliff and he looked at me like I was Sherlock Holmes, but I just pointed to his book as the giveaway clue and he laughed. I then started to ask him some questions about the things he'd love to do. (I can't help myself. It's just what I do.)

He started to talk about his emerging interest in commercial real estate. Cliff said it just lit him up. The more he dug into the subject, the more he got excited about it. He had a great big smile... and it kept on growing as he talked about the possibilities.

Then I asked him where he thought he'd like to live. In a nanosecond, he said, "Ohhhhhh, Atlanta. I've always wanted to try living there. It just looks like a great city. Plus, it's growing like crazy. I think it would be great."

My next question was, "Do you know anyone who lives in Atlanta?"

He said, "I have a friend or two... but no one who is in commercial real estate."

I said, "Okay... that's a start."

Just then they announced our flight would be delayed for a few more minutes.

That update inspired me.

I looked around and then I swung back to my new friend.

I said, "It sounds like we're going to be here for a while. Would you be willing to do a little experiment with me?"

His eyes narrowed. I think he was hit with feelings of fear and excitement all at the same time.

I said, "I don't know anyone in Atlanta in commercial real estate either... but you just never know who's sitting around us right now. You just never know whether someone right next to you might be holding a piece of the puzzle you need. So would you try something with me?"

We had talked a little about perfectionism in our conversation earlier... and how the fear of failing... or looking silly... could lock you up. So I spoke to that. I said, "Hey, I know there is a risk of looking like a dork right now. But the upside is... you'll probably never see any of these people again in your life. So if there's ever a time to make a mistake or look a little foolish... it's now."

He smiled and said, "Okay... let's do it."

I said, "Let's just see if anyone close by can help us out."

Now... I have to offer a caveat here. I've done this type of experiment numerous times. Sometimes it works out. Other times... it doesn't. But in this case... BAM... we got results quickly.

I turned to a young woman sitting at our shared table. She had been participating in our conversation from time to time... so I knew she was "good people," but I wasn't entirely sure how she'd react to my question. But I asked anyway.

I said, "Excuse me," and she looked up from working

on her laptop. She smiled curiously and said, "Yes?" I continued, "I'm not sure if you've heard the last part of our conversation, but my new friend, Cliff, is getting ready for his senior year in college and he's looking for an internship this summer. He has a growing interest in commercial real estate. More specifically, he goes to college in the midwest but he'd love to find a position in Atlanta. I know it's a long shot, but I'm trying to prove a point that you just never know who's sitting right next to you. Do you happen to know anyone in commercial real estate that lives in Atlanta?"

At first she laughed and Cliff wasn't sure how to react. I had a feeling we were on track, so I waited for what she was going to say next. She then said, "Well, I do have a friend in Atlanta. He's a great guy. I know him really well. Ironically, he has his own commercial real estate office. I can't make any promises, but I'd be happy to connect you with him. Maybe you could do an informational interview with him just to talk about the industry and the area. I'd be happy to make the introduction if you'd like."

Both Cliff and I couldn't believe it.

A solid connection... first try.

She gave him her card and said, "Follow up with me

and I'll connect you."

At that point, the gate agent started to announce the flight was ready, so our friend with the connection folded up her laptop and started to board. We thanked her for her openness to our *weirdness* and for her willingness to help Cliff out.

She was gracious and said she was happy to do it.

As Cliff and I were getting ready to board, he just kept smiling and saying, "I can't believe that!" I said, "You can't believe what?" He responded, "I would have never done that. I would have never asked someone I didn't know to help me." I replied, "I get it. Most wouldn't. Sometimes it's because we don't want to be a burden. Other times it's that we don't want to impose. But most of the time it's that we don't want to look silly or like we don't have it all together."

Many of us don't ask for help... because we don't want to appear less than perfect.

In this case, Cliff got over his perfectionist tendencies... the fear of looking like he needed help... the fear of looking silly... and he found a connection that made all the difference for him.

Fun stuff.

Okay... let's fast forward a year so I can offer...

EXAMPLE... part 2.

About twelve months after our chance meeting at O'Hare, I was asked to come speak at J.T. and Cliff's campus. (Believe it or not... I spoke on the subject of Dream Jobs. Shocker... right?)

While I was on campus I was able go grab some pizza with J.T. and Cliff and get caught up on their journey. While we were walking to the restaurant, I asked how things had gone with the connection we'd made in the airport. Cliff was excited to tell me that he'd not only followed up with her but he'd done the informational interview with her friend. That turned into an interview for an internship. Which all led to him moving to Atlanta for a full-time, paid internship in commercial real estate.

I was blown away. I joked with Cliff that I wish all my random connections at airports worked out that way... and he laughed.

Then I asked how it had gone. Specifically, I said, "Did you love it?"

He looked from side to side... almost as if to make

sure no one else was listening. Then he replied with, "It was okay. But it went a lot differently than I thought." I said, "How so?" He explained that he'd thought he'd really like the sales side of the industry... but when he got into it, he realized it wasn't what he expected.

His countenance shifted as he relayed this update.

In fact, Cliff shared this part of the update as if he had failed. But I think I'd surprised him with my response. I said, "That's awesome."

He looked at me weird. (I get that a lot.)

And then he said, "Why is that awesome?"

I said, "It's awesome because you figured out what you DON'T like. That's just as important as figuring out what you DO like."

I continued, "Now, let me ask... did you find anything that you really enjoyed doing?"

That's when his eyes lit up again. His big smile came back and he started to relay how he'd been really surprised at how much he enjoyed the technical parts of the transactions. He loved the logistics of it all. He loved putting the puzzle pieces together to make a deal happen. He loved the behind the scenes.

I said, "See? Now THAT is awesome. It was tempting to look at it like it was a failure, because it went different than you thought it was going to. But it was a HUGE win... because you figured out what you like and what you don't like."

Cliff nodded his head in agreement and said, "You're right. That is a win."

> *SIDE NOTE: Cliff has since graduated and is now working a Dream Job in commercial real estate in Chicago. He's helping to make big deals happen and staying in his sweet spot by bringing all the puzzle pieces together on deals all over the Windy City.*

Cliff learned to push through some of the traps of perfectionism:

- Waiting until things are perfect
- Not asking for help... because you're afraid of looking silly
- Feeling stuck because you don't want to fail

He took some chances. He asked for help. He tried some new things.

He learned. He stretched. He grew.

How about you?

What if you gave yourself permission to "fail" once in a while?

What might happen?

Now... as we wrap up this chapter... I want to give you one last tip.

If the thought of failing still makes you cringe a bit... let's put some guard rails on failure... especially when it comes to your career.

Let me ask my earlier question in a slightly different way.

What if you gave yourself permission to fail **LIKE A SCIENTIST?**

Think about it.

When a scientist enters a lab to do an experiment, they come in with a hypothesis. They start with an "educated guess" at how something is going to go. Then they experiment to see if their hypothesis is right.

If the experiment goes as planned... great.

If the experiment goes different than they had planned... great.

Either outcome is a win... because they're learning.

So go into any situation where you're going to stretch yourself... where you're going to try something new... where you're going to experiment... like a scientist.

In fact, let the "Two L's of Science" guide you.

What are the "Two L's of Science," you ask?

Learn fast.
Limit risk.

Learn fast:
Try new things and learn from them.

Try something and ask yourself questions like:

- What did I enjoy?
- What didn't I like about it?
- What would I want to do again?
- What would I change?

- How could I do more of that?
- How could I avoid doing that again?

Limit risk:

Find small but significant ways to experiment with something.

Don't quit your job to take a big blind leap to start a new career. Start smaller with taking a night class or an online course. Don't cash in your 401K to start a business from scratch. Start smaller with a side-hustle and experiment with ways to build the business as you have other income still coming in.

Don't just switch majors to something completely new overnight. Take some time to reach out to people doing the work you think you want to do. Ask them to coffee and find out about their day-to-day life. Learn more from people doing the work.

Although I'll be the first one to tell you to pursue your next Dream Job... I'm not a big fan of blind leaps of faith.

I am, however, a huge fan of "small steps of faith" over time.

So... push through those perfectionist tendencies.

Don't wait for perfect.

Ask for help.

Be willing to make some mistakes.

Be ready to fail once and awhile.

As you do... learn fast and limit risk.

There might be a few bumps along the way but it will make for one heck of an awesome ride!

NOTES:

Chapter Seven

G - GOALS

You've been dreaming.

You've been experimenting.

(Maybe you've even failed a few times... which will make you more successful!)

Now it's time to set some Magnetic Goals™.

Before, it was hard to know what you wanted and what it might take to achieve these things.

But now... after thinking back and looking forward... after thinking of possible Bridge Jobs and clues, after giving yourself permission to dream and experiment... you're more prepared to set some goals.

So let's talk "Magnetic Goals."

Magnetic Goals are goals you set that draw you to them. They're clear and compelling. You're hungry for them. They propel you towards a future you want!

They are... magnetic.

Also... Magnetic Goals are what we call... "informed goals."

There's thought behind them. They're not whims. They're not, as my Grandma Matthews would say, "passing fancies." They're not just, "I heard about an idea this morning and I'm going to quit my job now and do it," endeavors.

You've gone through a process.
You've come up with a list.
You're being intentional.

So... yes... Magnetic Goals start by being informed.

But what truly makes these goals "magnetic" is that you also understand the "why" behind them.

The "why" is key.

For example, I was working with one of my coaching clients. We had gone through the process you've just been learning about. We had talked about the "clues" in his life. As we did, we figured out more of his strengths and passions. Then we took the step of dreaming. He gave himself permission to think about the things he wanted more of in his life. Then we started to shift into planning and goal setting.

Now, this wasn't the first time he'd set some "work-life" balance goals. He'd read books. He'd been to a seminar. He had researched various strategies for time management. But nothing had stuck. Nothing had helped. So although he wanted this to be one of his big goals, he was anxious because he didn't want to fail.

I knew this was important for him. And I really wanted to make it stick. So I asked him one of the most important questions I can ask when I want to make a goal "magnetic."

I asked, "Why is this important to you... now?"

We were talking over the phone, so I didn't get to see his reaction. But the silence on the line let me know he was taking this question to heart. In fact, his voice cracked slightly as he replied. This hardened, successful executive quietly said, "My daughter is a junior in high school this year. Next year, she's a senior. After that she's off to college and who knows after that. I have two years to get this right. If I do... then I'm guessing we'll be really connected and have a great relationship the rest of her life. But if I miss this next two years... I'm guessing..." and he got quiet again, "I'm guessing I'll miss the rest of her life. And I *really* don't want that."

I let that sit for a minute and then responded, "Okay... that's a powerful why. Thanks for being willing to share it. Let's figure out some small steps you can start doing right now to make it happen."

He agreed. And we went after it.

We first set some bigger goals of what a great relationship and true work-life balance would look like. One of the best ways to quantify this was by setting a goal of taking a family vacation together in one year, where he could be 100% engaged and distraction-free, and they could have fun as a family for 7 days.

[NOTE: There are a lot of different ways you could set a goal around this type of broader goal, but this is one way to have a quantifiable target. Plus, it gave us one thing to work towards while also providing numerous opportunities for experimenting and learning. So this was one Magnetic Goal we landed on.]

In this case, the target was a 100% engaged, distraction-free and fun 7-day family vacation within the year.

You always want to break down a Magnetic Goal into smaller steps.

Some of the milestones we established were things like:

- Working together as a family to pick a destination
- Taking a few shorter trips as a family (1 to 2 days) where he could practice completely disengaging from work (this took discipline AND it took the cooperation from his team at work because they were VERY accustomed to being able to reach him at any time)
- Deciding to exercise as a family because they decided to take a vacation that was going to involve a lot of activities

We also wanted to establish some individual tasks that were completely dependent on my client. Experiments he could do that would allow him to work towards this Target via small but significant steps over time.

Some of these Individual Tasks were things like:

- Starting to block out 15 minutes a day to practice being really present and distraction

free
- Setting a goal of being home by 6 pm two nights a week (Remember: small steps. This eventually grew to 4 nights by the end of the year.)
- Completely turning off his phone at 8 pm two nights a week (He started to love the freedom this created, so this expanded too.)
- Doing some research on vacation destinations (He also reminded himself to not "bulldoze the family" with his ideas and encouraged everyone to bring ideas. They eventually went with an idea his daughter had suggested.)
- Experiment with time blocking and batching of tasks during the day

I'll be the first one to admit that each experiment didn't go smoothly. Some crashed and burned. Plus, it took a while for his family to get on board with the idea of a family vacation, since other trips had been cut short so he could return to the office to put out a fire. But as he kept talking about the vision of a distraction-free vacation and why it was important to him... and they could see that he was trying new things... everyone started to support the idea. They also had more grace for him as he bumbled through trying new things.

I'm happy to report my client was able to take a

100% distraction-free trip with his family (he didn't take a laptop and he didn't check email once) within the year. And even though there were still Clark-Griswold-level gaffs in their travel planning, the trip drew his family closer together and it helped them to launch into his daughter's senior year... just as he'd hoped.

Magnetic Goals:
Dreams with a <u>compelling plan</u> and a <u>clear why</u>.

So let's help you set some Magnetic Goals using the model I just walked you through. (It was subtle. Did you see it?)

That's right.

There's a planning tool I love that will help you to build a plan.

It's called the "I.M.T. Planning Tool."

That's right. "I.M.T."

Have you ever heard of "T.M.I.?"

I'm betting so.

As you probably know, T.M.I. Is short for "Too Much Information."

Maybe you have that "T.M.I." friend. The one who shares TOO much of the story. The one who sees the line and goes right over it... when it comes to relationships, work, or medical issues. Yow.

Yup... that's T.M.I.

TOO much info.

But the I.M.T. Planning Tool actually helps you get to the right information.

T = TARGET
M = MILESTONES
I = INDIVIDUAL TASKS

TARGET

The Target is your bigger goal in a given area.

It might be to run a marathon, get a promotion, start a company, lose 25 pounds or... take a distraction-free vacation with your family.

For the purposes of illustration, we'll use the example of having a Target of running the Chicago Marathon.

MILESTONES

These are tasks that sometimes involve other people and always involve completion dates. They serve as mile markers that help us track our progress and keep our momentum.

In our Chicago Marathon example... let's say it's April and we want to run the Chicago Marathon in October. Some of our Milestones could be:

- Find a training partner by May 1
- Find a training schedule you like by July 1
- Run in a 10K race by August 15
- Run a half-marathon by September 12

INDIVIDUAL TASKS

These are are small but significant steps that are completely up to the individual.

For example, in our Chicago Marathon scenario, some Individual Tasks would be:

- Sign up for the marathon (Yup... THAT is important!)
- Buy some new running shoes (Gotta have the look!)
- Start running and following a plan
- Find a running diet you like

I often find it helpful to create a chart and list my Target, Milestones, and some of my top Individual Tasks. Then I keep that chart close by to help me to stay on track.

The I.M.T. Planning Tool™:

Individual Tasks	Milestones	Target
Specific tasks that are up to you as an individual.	Tasks that involve completion dates and/or other people.	Your bigger goal.

MAGNETIC GOAL QUESTIONS:

Here are some questions to help guide you as you start to build your plan. For the sake of "experimenting" with the I.M.T. Tool, pick one to three dreams from your list to take through this process.

TARGET QUESTIONS:

- Of all of the dreams you have written down so far, which do you want to focus on over the next year?
- Which career-related dream do you want to build a plan for?
- Which other dreams do you want to focus on?

MILESTONE QUESTIONS:

- What are some possible milestones to help you hit this Target?
- Who could help you go after this Target?

INDIVIDUAL TASKS:

- What are some small but significant steps you might take to achieve this Target?
- What might be the best sequence for these steps?
- Which of these tasks seem to be the most important right now?

WHY-RELATED QUESTIONS:

- In order to make a dream "magnetic," we need to get clear on why it's important for you.
- So for each dream you build a plan for, ask at

least one of the following:
- Why is this dream important to you right now?
- Who else will this dream positively impact?
- What could you learn from pursuing this dream?
- How could you benefit from achieving this dream?

Have some fun with this.

Take some time and experiment with the I.M.T. Planning Tool.

Just see where it takes you!

[And remember... it doesn't need to be perfect!!!]

NOTES:

Chapter Eight

H - HELP

It's okay to ask for help.

In fact... when you're on the road to a dream career, it's required.

> *"Don't be shy about asking for help. It doesn't mean you're weak. It only means you're wise."*
> - Author Unknown

We can't do this alone.

We need help when we're charting a new path.

We need encouragement, wisdom, and assistance with the heavy lifting. This is especially true when we're going against the norm to find work we love and to create a life we actually want.

So... yeah... when you're either creating or finding a Dream Job, you're going to need...

M.M.A.

No. Not Mixed Martial Arts... although that might not hurt. :)

When I say "M.M.A." I mean... Masterminds, Mentors, and Allies.

MASTERMINDS:

Napoleon Hill is credited with coining the concept of "Mastermind Groups" in his book, *Think and Grow Rich*. He wrote the book in the 1930s after interviewing the most successful business people of that era. As a result, he identified a number of shared traits and strategies that were common within their journeys. One concept was the idea of meeting with a small group of people on a regular basis in order to help and push each other forward.

Hill called it the "Mastermind Principle."

> *"Two or more people actively engaged in the pursuit of a definite purpose with a positive mental attitude, constitute an unbeatable force."*
> - Napoleon Hill

As a result, successful people started to meet in small groups with the express goal of helping one another to get clarity, encourage each other, and achieve more. They called them "Mastermind Groups."

I first heard about this concept when I was meeting with people and trying to learn as much as I could about entrepreneurship. A number of successful business people told me about how they made time to do this on a regular basis. The format looked different from group to group, but the themes of meeting on a regular basis, creating a safe space, accountability and encouragement seemed to be consistent. Once I started to hear about this idea, I knew I wanted something like it.

I started to experiment. I tried to start different groups. Some sparked but then fizzled. Some went a little sideways. Some just never really got off the ground. But then in 2007... a group of like-minded friends and I started a group. They were successful entrepreneurs in similar fields to mine. So I knew we could learn from each other and push each other but also not feel like we were competing either.

As we began to meet on a regular basis, we decided we needed a name. So, we called our crew "Mesh." The reason why was a little goofy, actually. I'd joked that we should all wear uniforms to the meetings. The idea got batted around... as those things do. Someone suggested "mesh half-shirts" in all the back and forth banter. (YIKES!)

Then... even though we never took that fashion advice... the name "Mesh" just stuck. #dorks

We've been meeting ever since.

The format has evolved and changed over the years. In the beginning we'd meet every other week. We'd present our plans, vet new ideas, lament about setbacks and celebrate the wins. I know that my company and my life have grown significantly thanks to the regular encouragement, wisdom, and accountability I've received from these guys.

Initially, I thought "Mastermind Groups" were limited more to entrepreneurs, but as I did more of my Dream Job Interviews, I found these types of stories popped up in many of their lives. They didn't always call them "Masterminds," but the people with Dream Jobs I interviewed had intentionally surrounded themselves with some like-minded people who encouraged them to stay on track.

Sometimes this meant face-to-face meetings. In other cases it meant video chats and FaceTime sessions with friends in other parts of the world. It might not have been every two weeks like clockwork, but I consistently heard stories of people meeting with others for the express purpose of propelling each other forward.

The frameworks may vary, but the flavor is the same.

There are a lot of different ways to apply Hill's Mastermind Principle, but here's a system that works for many... including MESH.

TIMING:

You'll need to find a schedule that works for your group. It might be once every two weeks or once a month. Experiment to see what works best. The key is that you need to meet on a regular basis to maximize the power of the Mastermind.

You'll also need to decide on how long you meet because this will have an impact on how you spend your time when you're together.

I encourage groups to include these core elements:

- Time to connect
- Time for each person to share
- Time to lock in logistics for your next session

For my group, there are three of us and we typically meet for two hours. So this is how our time breaks down.

TWO HOUR MASTERMIND SESSION:

- We eat for 25 minutes and catch up on life
- Person 1 - 30 minutes
- Person 2 - 30 minutes
- Person 3 - 30 minutes
- 5 minutes to confirm next meeting time

During our 30 minutes, we focus on the following questions:

MASTERMIND SESSION QUESTIONS:

- What is going well?
- What needs to be tweaked?
- Where are you feeling stuck and/or where do you need some help?
- What do you want to have done by the next time we meet?

We do watch the clock... and the last 5 minutes of anyone's 30 minute time block is dedicated to answering that last question. "What do you want to have done by the next time we meet?"

That way we have clarity and direction. Plus, we know what to be asking about and checking in on the rest of the month.

Now, I will say, we put a high priority on having fun and encouraging each other, so we do joke around... especially during the first 25 minutes. Plus, these guys will be the first ones to encourage me during tough times or when I experience a setback. BUT they'll also be the first ones to call me out if I don't do what I say I'm going to do. And they'll be first in line to kick my butt if it seems like I'm not pushing myself enough.

It's been a game changer for me.

If you don't have the Mastermind Principle working in your life... I hope you give it a try.

I did a full DREAM THINK DO Podcast episode on this subject.

You can check it out at MitchMatthews.com/120.

MENTORS:

The concept of mentorship has been around for a very long time, but some of the concepts we'll touch on here have only been possible in the last decade or so.

We're going to talk about Long-Term Mentors, Snapshot Mentors, and e-Mentors.

men·tor

ˈmenˌtôr,ˈ

noun

1. an experienced and trusted adviser.

The idea is to seek out a person who has gone before you.

To find someone you can learn from... someone who will share insights and ask questions.

> "*Show me a successful individual and I'll show you someone who had real positive influences in their life. I don't care what you do for a living - if you do it well I'm sure there was someone cheering you on or showing the way. A mentor.*"
> - Denzel Washington

Now... in some cases... a mentor relationship may look like meeting with the same person for an extended amount of time. I call this a "Long-Term

Mentor." In others, it might mean you meet with someone once but you're able to learn something from them that helps you gain some valuable perspective. I call this a "Snapshot Mentor."

LONG-TERM MENTOR

I came across a great example of a "Long-Term Mentor" relationship when I interviewed Don Yaeger, the Associate Editor for Sports Illustrated magazine. Over his career, Don has had the pleasure of meeting and interviewing some of the biggest names in sports. Michael Jordan, Jimmy Johnson, Phil Mickelson, Serena Williams and Mia Hamm... just to name a few.

If they've made an impact on sports in the last 30 years, there's a good chance Don has spent time with them.

In one instance, Don was interviewing John Wooden, the most successful coach in NCAA Men's Basketball history. (He won 10 NCAA titles in a 12 year period!) During their conversation, the subject of mentors came up. Coach Wooden shared some insights that sparked an idea for Don.

So days later, Yaeger reached back out and asked if Dr. Wooden would consider mentoring him. It was a bold ask. In fact, Don said he almost didn't do it because with all of Coach's success, Yaeger figured he was approached like this on a weekly basis. As it turned out, Wooden was delighted by the request and told him to come to his home the following week. That started a TEN YEAR mentor relationship that involved monthly marathon sessions where Coach poured out stories, strategies, and wisdom. Plus he took time to answer every question Don brought.

Can you imagine?

What an experience.

What a gift.

One of the things I love most about that story was that Don later talked to Coach Wooden about how he almost hadn't asked because he assumed he would get requests like that all the time. The wise coach joked and explained a lot of people must assume that so he was rarely asked. Don was shocked. He was also very glad he'd pushed through the fear and made the request.

[You can listen to my full interview with Don here: MitchMatthews.com/126.]

Who's someone you would love to have as a mentor?

What if you asked?

If you'd like to get a Long-Term Mentor, my suggestion is... don't propose marriage on the first date.

What I mean is, if you have someone you think you might want to have as a Long-Term Mentor... don't make that your first ask. Instead, start smaller. Keep it simple. Begin with more of a "Snapshot Mentor" relationship in mind.

SNAPSHOT MENTOR

A "Snapshot Mentor" is someone who's willing to spend a short amount of time with you to help you in a specific area. It might be 15 minutes or it could be a longer session over coffee or lunch.

But it's a shorter time period with a low level of commitment.

Whether you're shooting for a "Long-term Mentor" or a "Snapshot Mentor," I suggest you remember **G.E.T.** when you reach out.

GREETING

If you're going to make your initial contact via email, start with a warm greeting. Too many people write emails as if they are a text message. They cut right to the request with no setup. If you're going to be reaching out and making an "ask" like this, you want to start by letting them know you hope their day is going great. A simple, "I hope you're doing great today," will do. But if you want to go a little deeper into something that might be unique to the recipient... you can speak to the weather, something about the city they live in, and/or mention the last time you saw them. This helps the person see that you've put some thought into the email, you're human AND that this is not some sort of form letter you're using over and over.

ENCOURAGEMENT

I suggest offering a compliment. Something specific. Tell them about something they've done or said that inspired you and/or helped you in some way. Let them know how it impacted you and thank them for it.

If you're reaching out to a leader in the organization where you currently work, you might share a story of a time where you were impacted by a presentation they'd made, helped by an insight they'd shared in the hallway or impressed by a project they'd helped to lead.

If you're reaching out to a thought leader or an author, offer some specific encouragement on how something they included in their book, shared in an interview and/or said during a speech made an impact. Go even further and share an example of how you'd changed a behavior because of it and/or applied the concept.

Sure, there's the chance it might look like you're sucking up, but I've found that if a compliment is made from an authentic place, it's usually received in an authentic way too.

TIME

Then after you include your warm greeting and a little encouragement, you can ask for time.

If you don't know the person, ask for a 15 minute phone call.

Say you really want to respect their time and you have a few questions you would like to ask them.

This might sound like a stretch... but J.T. used this approach to score his Dream Job.

I'd mentioned meeting Cliff in the O'Hare airport in the chapter on failing.

Well, J.T. was his buddy who was sitting next to him when I started to talk with them about their Dream Jobs. As we chatted, Cliff had shared about getting into commercial real estate... and if you remember, we were able to help him make a great connection right there as we all waited for our plane.

J.T.'s story didn't play out that fast.

When I asked J.T. about the work he'd love to do, he started to tell me about Fox Racing. He'd ridden and raced motorcycles all of his life and he'd always used Fox Racing equipment for his bike. He loved their innovative approach, their excellence and their commitment to the sport.

J.T. lit up as he talked about them.

(Ironically, his last name and the company's name are the same... but there's no relation.)

I asked if he knew anyone inside the company, but he didn't. I assured him that was okay and we started to talk about taking the "Snapshot Mentor" approach. To find people inside the organization and to ask for a quick call. Just 15 minutes for a few specific questions.

Although I think he had his doubts... he agreed to try the strategy.

He started to look for potential connections online. LinkedIn. Facebook. Instagram. In fact, his first connection was someone who raced for Fox he found via his Instagram profile. J.T. reached out. Greeted him warmly. Said he was impressed with some of his pics and his stats. And then he asked for 15 minutes of time. The racer obliged.

They got on the phone. J.T. asked his questions and he authentically listened. The racer started talking. So much so... at the 13-minute mark, J.T. interrupted and said, "I'm sorry. I asked for 15 minutes and we're getting close to that. Is it okay if we go a little longer?" His new friend was halfway through a good story and was quick to say, "Heck yes," before continuing on.

That first call lasted an hour.

Thanks to one of the questions I'll share with you, that call also led to another call with someone else in the company... and another... and another. These calls and some additional follow up eventually led to a personal tour of Fox Racing's corporate headquarters for J.T.

Crazy cool.

In fact, in less than two years after our chance encounter in Chicago O'Hare, I was able to do an interview with J.T. about HIS Dream Job. The best part of that interview was that he made the call from the back deck of Fox Racing HQ... because... yeah... that's where he works now.

That's right.

His efforts had paid off.

Dream Job... accomplished.

[You can check out my convo with J.T. at MitchMatthews.com/041.]

So... let's review:

SNAPSHOT MENTOR:

A "Snapshot Mentor" is a person who offers insight and/or help in a short interaction. (For example, a brief chat, a phone call, a conversation over coffee or lunch.)

Snapshot Mentor Questions:

Here are a few questions I suggest asking a Snapshot Mentor.

Also, make special note of the "Next Step" questions that helped J.T. continue to connect with more and more people at Fox Racing:

- What do you enjoy about your work?
- What surprised you about your job?
- What do you wish you would have known before you started?
- If I was interested in doing what you do, what would you suggest I read or learn about?
- **NEXT STEP QUESTIONS:**
    - Who else should I be talking to?
    - Would you be willing to introduce us?

Since J.T. was in Ohio and Fox Racing was in California, he needed to make most of these connections over the phone. You might be able to walk across the hall at work to meet with someone you'd like to be learning from.

And, if you invited them and your meeting involves food or beverages... honor them and offer to pay. If a lunch is too expensive, keep it to coffee. They might not let you pay, but offer any way. It's the right thing to do.

Lastly, if your Snapshot Mentor session goes well, you can consider asking the person if they would be interested in becoming a Long-Term Mentor for you.

Start small.

See where it takes you.

Okay... so that's Long-Term Mentors and Snapshot Mentors.

Now, before we leave the subjects of mentoring, let's touch briefly on something I call "e-Mentors."

e-Mentor:

This is not something that would have been an option a generation ago, but it's an incredibly powerful tool. It won't cost you a penny. You won't have to worry about schedules (yours or your mentor's). You can use it to amass a ton of wisdom, insight and strategy. You can really get to know your e-Mentor. Plus, you don't have to wait for anyone's permission to get started.

And... most importantly... you can begin right now.

The idea is that you pick a thought leader. [It helps if they have written a book and/or taught on a specific subject you're interested in.]

Then you study that person's work... for 10 days.

You can certainly read any books or articles they have written, but I prefer to spend time with my e-Mentors while I'm moving. So when I'm driving, exercising... or even mowing the lawn... I'll hit iTunes and search to see if they have done any podcast interviews. Then I'll do a Google search to see if there are any talks or discussions on YouTube.

If they've written a book, there's a very good chance they'll have done a number of interviews to promote it and they'll tend to cover the main points in a 30-minute conversation. If I'm able to listen to several of those over the course of a week to 10 days, I'll understand many of their most important concepts, remember their best stories, and be ready to apply some of the key strategies. [I might even listen to the same interview multiple times to make sure I caught everything!]

It's as if I am able to sit down with them and learn from them directly... but I can do it when it works for me. And I don't even have to buy the person a venti skinny vanilla latte. Pretty sweet deal.

If you're needing some ideas for some e-Mentors, here are a few of my favorite e-Mentor strategies.

- Google the phrase "Thought leaders in _____" and fill in the blank with something you're interested in
    - Once you have your list, hit the iTunes podcast section and search for each person
    - Find someone with a number of interviews and BANG... you have your first e-Mentor
    - Start digging in
- Google the phrase "Best interviews of all time" and watch some of those (the results change all the time and many will #blowyourmind)
    - Find someone you resonate with and Google that person
    - Also search the iTunes podcast section for that person and... BOOM! You've got yourself another e-Mentor!

- Get to it
- Hit TED.com and search any subject you're interested in
  - Start watching and find a speaker you like
  - Start digging in to Google, YouTube, and iTunes for them
  - POW... e-Mentors abound!
- Hit Amazon.com and search the bookstore for a subject you're interested in
  - Take a look at the most popular books on the subjects
  - When you find a book/author who intrigues you, start checking out iTunes and Google... cuz BLAP... you might just have yourself another e-Mentor!

Simple idea.

Powerful.

Cheap.

Fast.

And... something your Grandpa wasn't able to do when he was thinking about HIS Dream Job.

Thank you, internet.

[I covered this concept in an episode of DREAM THINK DO, you can check out here: MitchMatthews.com/125.]

ALLIES

Finally, we come to the subject of Allies... and being intentional about who you surround yourself with.

> *"There's nothing like a really loyal, dependable, good friend. Nothing."*
> - Jennifer Aniston

Allies are a specific type of friend.

Allies laugh with you... not at you. Allies encourage you and at the same time shoot straight with you if you need a little course correction. Allies want what is best for you and they celebrate with you when you get it. Allies aren't perfect... and they don't expect you to be perfect either.

Allies are key. We need them in our lives.

> *"It is better to be alone than in bad company."*
> - George Washington

You have to make time for Allies.

I'm wildly blessed to say that my wife is an amazing Ally for me. She encourages me and stands by me. She pushes and supports me. And... I do my best to do the same for her!

If you're married... I hope the same for you.

I also have an Ally I've met with once a week for about 10 years straight. We meet at 6 am on Friday mornings at a local coffee shop. It's located halfway between our houses. We've sat in the same chairs about 48 weeks out of every year. So that means we've had about 480 cups of java together.

In truth, years ago we lived closer to each other and we had initially started meeting early in the morning to work out at a local gym. We'd both wanted to get into shape and we knew we needed the accountability. However, one morning the gym was closed due to some remodeling, so we went to a diner across the street instead. Then we realized we seemed to get way more out of some quality coffee and good conversation than we did from exercising.

So we stayed with the coffee. #Lifegoals

That time has provided a lot of laughs and some great memories. But it's also helped me through some of the toughest times in my career. Times when I didn't believe in myself. Times when things looked pretty bleak. That Ally has pushed me to keep on track towards my goals and I'd like to think I've done that for him too.

> *"Keep away from people who try to belittle your ambitions. Small people always do that, but the really great make you feel that you, too, can become great."*
> - Mark Twain

Find those Allies in your life.

Make time for them.

And if you don't have any currently... hang in there.

Look for opportunities to be that kind of Ally for others... and I'm guessing they'll start to appear in your life too!

MASTERMIND, MENTORS, and ALLIES QUESTIONS:

Who would you want to try to start a Mastermind group with?

Who are some people you want to reach out to as possible Long-Term Mentors and/or Snapshot Mentors?

Where could you start to apply the e-Mentor strategy in your life?

Who are some Allies in your life you want to make some time for in the next two weeks?

NOTES:

Chapter Nine

I - INTENTIONALITY

Intentionality is the linchpin to this process.

linch·pin
'lin(t)SHpin/
noun

Definition of linchpin
1: a locking pin inserted crosswise (as through the end of an axle or shaft)
2: one that serves to hold together parts or elements that exist

Linchpins are not used in modern design as much as they used to be. In days past, a linchpin would hold a wheel on a wagon in place. It would keep it from slipping off the axle.

[Source: https://www.merriam-webster.com/ dictionary/linchpin]

No linchpin = no progress.

Apparently, it used to be a common prank in the 17th and 18th centuries to pull the linchpin from an unsuspecting carriage owner. This act of tomfoolery would almost guarantee the carriage would go off the road in a most inconvenient (and often dangerous) way.

Can you imagine THAT family road trip?

18th century Clark Griswold and the family getting in their covered wagon to head home after a trip to see Grandma. An agrarian-age Cousin Eddy removes a linchpin... *just for fun.* And a mile and a half down the road... Clark and the family are in the ditch because the linchpin wasn't there. #notfunny

The linchpin is key.

It holds things together.

If it's in place... things stay on track.

If it's not there... things go funky quick.

Intentionality is the linchpin in attaining or creating a dream career.

Let's face it. Most people walk out their career by accident. They get an education by default. They pick a degree because someone suggested it or because a friend was doing it. They take that first job because it was offered and then they settle in. Promotions come because there was an opening. Then... before they know it... three decades have passed... they're full of regret... and that general feeling of "where did the time go?" gnaws at their heart.

I have a friend who calls these people the "Greys."

They walk around with dull-eyes... almost zombie-like.

They don't start out this way... but they took a job... not because they were excited about it, but because it was available. They told themselves they'd just stay in it for a while... until something better came along. A year or two passed. They bought some stuff. They got used to the income.

Then a promotion became available. It offered more responsibilities and an 11% increase in pay. They interviewed. As they did, they had a dull ache in their gut telling them it was a bad fit. They dismissed the feeling because it seemed like a logical progression. Plus, they had already started to think about what they'd do with that little extra cha-chinga each month.

Then... they got the position. The announcement was exciting. The new desk was fun. But within 3 weeks they knew they should have listened to their gut.

They start to notice a feeling of dread as they drive to work each morning. The work feels off. They're okay at the tasks, but they only enjoy a fraction of the things they do on a day-to-day basis. Six months in... they start to feel like a little piece of them is dying as they walk from their car to their desk each morning... but they're not sure how to fix it.

They suppress this awareness with a few binge sessions on Netflix, telling themselves they'll make a change soon. But then, a decade passes and they're a full-fledged "Grey"... barely awake... trying to remember a time when they were excited about their work.

Do you know anyone like this? I'm guessing you do.

Heck, I've been dangerously close to becoming a "Grey" myself.

Maybe you have too.

But hey... I know you.

You don't want that. That's not you.

You don't want to walk out a career based on what was available at the time.

You want to craft something.

You want to do something significant.

Not because it's easy.

Not because it's common.

But because it matters.

You want to learn, grow, earn, contribute... and live a freakishly awesome life.

Am I right?

Well... intentionality is at the core.

> *"Ultimately, human intentionality is the most powerful evolutionary force on the planet."*
> - George B. Leonard

It's critical.

In order to turn a "bad fit" job into a Bridge Job... you need to be intentional. You need to think about ways to apply the M.E.A.L. Plan.

Who can you MEET? What can you EARN? What might you be AVAILABLE to do? What might you LEARN?

To find meaningful CLUES, you have to be intentional, slow down and ask some important questions.

> *"Wanting to win isn't enough. You have to go through the process to improve. That takes patience, perseverance, and intentionality."*
> - John C. Maxwell

In order to DREAM... you have to be intentional. Much of the world will want to distract you or discourage you from figuring out what your dreams are and pursuing them. It's a part of human nature. That is one of the reasons you have to be so intentional.

You know this. Heck, that's why you're reading THIS

book. You know you need to fill your mind with stories, concepts, and strategies that will propel you forward. Sure. There are plenty of stories of people failing and falling short.

But because you dive into content like this... you also know that even though you'll experience setbacks on your journey towards your dreams, pushing through those ups and downs is what it takes to achieve an amazing life.

To stay motivated to EXPERIMENT and go after your GOALS... you need to be intentional.

> *"It takes courage to grow up and turn out to be who you really are."*
> - E.E. Cummings

You have to intentionally choose who you want to surround yourself with.

As we've discussed... you can't eliminate 100% of the jackweeds from your life... but you can bolster yourself by purposefully spending time with your Mentors and Allies.

> *"You don't climb mountains without a team, you don't climb mountains without being prepared, and you don't climb mountains without balancing the risks and rewards. And you NEVER climb a mountain by accident - it has to be intentional."*
> - Mark Udall

So... yes.

Intentionality is a linchpin.

You have to commit... and recommit.

Not because it's the norm.

But instead because you know living and working with intentionality is what it takes.

You can choose to break free from the Greys.

Granted... you may not be in a Dream Job currently, but try out that mantra:

> *"I'm either in a Dream Job or I'm working towards one. That's how I live."*

Make the choice... daily.

Live with intentionality.

It will make all the difference.

Amen?

Amen.

NOTES:

Chapter Ten

J - Job(s)

The term "Dream Job" has meant different things to different people.

For some in generations past, a Dream Job meant finding a good job and staying with it until you die or retire (whichever came first). That might have worked for some... but in our ever-changing-work-world... this approach is not really an option now.

For others, they equated the idea of a Dream Job with an unachievable "rainbows and butterflies" type utopia where nothing ever goes wrong and the work is always easy.

Since this seemed unrealistic and even silly... some put the concept of a Dream Job in the category of the Lochness Monster, Bigfoot and Unicorns. (Fun to think about... but not something you'd ever see yourself.)

For others still... they assume Dream Jobs might exist but they're only for people who:

- graduated in the top 2% of their class
- have always had 3% body fat
- went to an ivy league school
- have participated in the Olympics in TWO different sports!!
- have great hair

Since these folks believe Dream Jobs are only for the elite of the elite... they think it's not something us "normal" people can aspire to.

Well... I'd dare to suggest a different definition entirely.

That's right.

If you boil down all of the stories, interviews and examples of people who have achieved real Dream Jobs in today's world... a new definition for a Dream Job begins to emerge.

dream·job

dreem-job

noun

Definition of Dream Job

1: Doing work you love

2: And/or doing work that enables you to do something you love

You'll notice... this definition does not say anything about there just being ONE Dream Job for each person... and that once you find it, you'll need to stay in it the rest of your days.

Nope.

(Most of the people I've interviewed have had a series of Dream Jobs with some Bridge Jobs in between.)

This definition doesn't say the work will always be easy. (We talked about the potential for "Suck Factor" when we talked about the importance of Attitude.) Dream Jobs often involve hard work, long days and sometimes... even... risk.

BUT it's work you love. It's fulfilling. It's work that matters.

This definition says nothing about Dream Jobs being limited to the top scholars, international athletes, the social elite or those with great hair. This definition allows ALL of us to either find or create Dream Jobs that are just right for us.

The keys:

- We need to START
- We need to pay attention to the SEASONS
- We need to think "JOB(s)."

Let's dive into each of these final keys in more depth.

START:

When you think back on the examples we've covered so far... in every case, each person wasn't exactly sure what their Dream Job was when they started.

Many had an "essence" of what the Dream Job was when they began.

BUT they weren't 100% clear.

The key was they had to START in order to figure it out.

Sara Haines had to START as an NBC Page.

Antonio Neves had to START as a temp at Viacom.

Diego Corzo had to START by driving around a local

real estate agent.

Jon Vroman had to START by helping just one person.

Sam Griffin had to START by pushing through fear.

You can listen to their stories on the podcast here:
- Sara Haines: http://mitchmatthews.com/010
- Antonia Neves: http://mitchmatthews.com/004
- Diego Corzo: http://mitchmatthews.com/132
- Jon Vroman: http://mitchmatthews.com/034
- Sam Griffin: http://mitchmatthews.com/118

John's Story:

John Michael Morgan had to START... after he dropped out of college.

School just wasn't for John. It just never clicked with him.

It wasn't that he wasn't smart.

He just didn't like being confined to a classroom.

It wasn't for him.

In fact, on the first day of college, one of his

professors greeted the room with a warning. "This isn't high school. I'm not here to babysit you. In fact, if you get up right now and walk out... I won't stop you."

John can't tell you what the professor said next because he took him up on the offer. He walked out and never came back!

In my interview with John, he said,

"I didn't have a plan. I wasn't sure what I was going to do next. But at that point, I just knew what I didn't want."

So John started.

He'd be the first one to admit that he bumped around in life for a bit trying different things but then he started to experiment with real estate sales. The first few months didn't go well, but he stayed with it.

He started to learn. He began to dig into marketing and branding strategies that could help him sell more houses.

Although he'd never enjoyed school... he developed an insatiable desire to study. He started reading books, listening to CD's, and attending workshops.

John also started to apply the things he was learning and his real estate business began to explode. He kept learning. He kept applying the lessons. He kept winning. In fact, although he was the youngest agent in his area, he started to break sales record after sales record.

The phone started to ring with new clients.

But the phone also started to ring with people asking for his advice.

Ironically, this college dropout started to become the go-to expert on branding and marketing in his area. His real estate business continued to grow but he found that he was enjoying sharing and teaching business strategies even more than selling homes.

Then it happened.

He had been on the phone giving business advice to a friend. After getting done with the call, John's wife Brooke approached him. She pointed to the fact that he was really good at real estate, but he seemed to love branding and marketing even more. She also brought up that people from around the country were now calling him for his input on how to grow their businesses. That's when she suggested John start to experiment with building a business around his passion for branding and marketing.

So he did.

He started.

He didn't leave real estate immediately.

He started to build a branding agency on the side.

Over time his clientele started to grow. The income from his agency work started to eclipse his real estate work, and so he launched into it full time. Now, his client list includes companies like Disney and Starbucks as well as celebrities, churches and entrepreneurs.

He loves his work.

BUT he would have never found it... if he hadn't STARTED.

I want that for you.

I want you to love the work you're doing.

If you're not there... I want to encourage you to START.
No matter where you're at.

Whether you're 13, 23, 33, 43 or 73.

It's never too early.

It's never too late.

Start.

Take a step. Experiment. Try something new. Revisit something you used to do. Make that call. Take a class. Offer to help someone.

Don't wait until your 100% clear.

Clarity will come as you're on the journey.

So get started.

[To listen to this interview with John, go here: MitchMatthews.com/018.]

SEASONS:

Speaking of the "journey," one of the other things I've learned is different "seasons" of life will also open up new types of Dream Jobs.

For example, I interviewed Tom Pietras.

Tom is a successful executive with American Family Insurance.

He went to school to be in advertising. After college he joined an agency and really enjoyed the work of writing copy, guiding campaigns and working with clients. Those successes eventually led him to AmFam where he shot up through the ranks in the marketing department.

He'll be the first to say that his career has involved multiple Dream Jobs with a few Bridge Jobs mixed in from time to time.

Then a chance encounter sparked a entirely new Dream Job.

Tom had grown up playing the drums. His dad was a great drummer and taught his son the art and the science of not only keeping rhythm but also moving an audience. But then in his teens, an argument with his father caused Tom to put down his sticks for over three decades.

Then he attended a function at a local college. While there, he wound up sitting at a table of people he didn't know.

Over the course of the evening, the subject of music came up.

Tom mentioned his past love for drumming. A woman at the table (who he'd only met 20 minutes prior) mentioned her family had a drum set they no longer needed. She offered to loan it to him for 30 days to see if his skills and passion would return.

The idea of coming back to drumming had just started to knock on a door in Tom's heart, so he took her up on the offer. He set up the drums in his home and from the minute his foot hit the bass drum pedal and his stick tapped a cymbal... it all came back.

It was like he'd never stopped.

He was in his 50's but his teenage passion for percussion came rushing back.

Now, Tom didn't march in and quit his job as an executive.

Nope. He simply started to experiment.

First, he started to assemble a band. They were good.

They played at their church. They had fun.

They expanded their playlist and started to play locally.

They called themselves the "Ryan McGrath Band" (You can learn more here: http://www.theryanmcgrathband.com/) named after their lead singer. They found additional members. They worked hard.

Word started to spread.
Opportunities for gigs started to come in.

Tom still didn't quit his day job.

BUT... as notoriety for the band increased... and requests became more numerous... Tom made a decision. He decided to talk with his boss about this renewed passion and how things were starting to take shape with the band. He let management know that he was still very passionate about his work, but he wanted to explore making more time to pursue this new dream. As a result, he shifted roles into a position that allowed him to reduce his work load and his travel.

Instead of hiding it from his employer, he was open about his dream.

They supported it.

He committed to excellence but also let them know he would be working hard on this new dream on the side.

Granted, not every employer will respond this way. But many will... especially if you commit to delivering quality work and being fully engaged.

When I interviewed Tom, he was still fully employed in his "day job" which in many ways would also qualify as a Dream Job for him. But he was continuing to devote time to his "side job" which is also a Dream Job for him... and the effort paying off.

In the past few months, they've played before NFL games and at Harley Davidson's Headquarters. They even have opened for Darius Rucker and Jennifer Hudson. Plus, most weekends you can catch the band playing gigs in front of packed houses at various top tier brew houses and watering holes in the Midwest.

Try to catch a show. You'll be glad you did. The music will get your toe tapping... and I guarantee Tom's big smile from behind the drum set will make you grin too!

[You can check out my interview with Tom at MitchMatthews.com/109.]

Seasons.

Tom said that if the opportunity to drum had come earlier in his career, it wouldn't have been the right time. It wouldn't have been a good fit. It wouldn't have worked.

But since it came when it did... he was able to pursue it.

It was the right season.

I bring this up because it's important.

In fact... this concept is freeing.

I think some people resist the idea of a "Dream Job" because they think that once they've found it... they'll need to stay in that for the rest of their days.

As a result, they feel like they have to get it right.

If they don't, they might get stuck.

But that's horse scat.

It's just not what I've seen in all the interviews I've done.

What I've seen time and time again... is that different seasons bring different priorities and different opportunities.

Give yourself permission to think about what your Dream Job might be for this season. Then give yourself permission to think (and dream) about what your Dream Job might look like for future seasons.

Know that it will evolve.

It will change.

The fact that your idea of a Dream Job will shift over time doesn't make you flaky. It doesn't mean your indecisive or wishy-washy.

It means you're not limiting yourself to just one.

It means you're intentionally designing a career that will include MULTIPLE Dream Jobs!

How cool is that?

DREAM JOB(s)

Adding the "S" to Dream Job to make it plural is very important.

I don't want you to just have one in your career.

I want you to have multiple Dream Jobs.

We've already talked about how the seasons of our lives will shape our perception of what a Dream Job is.

Plus... I've learned... Dream Jobs tend to have what I call "hidden back doors." So one Dream Job will often lead to another.

These back doors are hidden because you only find them when you're doing the work. They're hidden because you only find them as you move forward. They're hidden because you don't tend to know they exist when you first start on your journey.

My first experience with a "hidden back door" came with I was 14.

As you can tell by now... I've always been a bit of an extreme person. That's just who I am. It's always been that way.

"Extreme" is one way to put it. "Weird" is another.

Well, when I was 12, my whole world was bicycles. I read about them. I talked about them. I loved them. Since, I lived in a small town in Iowa, I rode bikes everywhere. As a result, my idea of a Dream Job at that age was to work at the little hole-in-the-wall bike shop in town.

It was called "Marty's Schwinn Cyclery" and I spent as much time there as I could. With the smell of WD40 in the air, posters of professional cyclists on the walls as well as new bikes everywhere... it was heaven for me.

I'd try to do odd jobs around the shop just so Marty (the owner) and the other employees wouldn't get sick of me. I'd sweep the sidewalk. I'd wipe down the bikes. I'd even slip over and mow Marty's lawn on hot summer days. I did it so I wouldn't get kicked out. But I also did it with the hopes that someday I could score a job.

Then... at age 13... it happened. I'll never forget it. Marty's wife Cheri asked to talk with my parents. I wasn't sure why. I thought I might be in trouble. Maybe she was going to drop the hammer and ask my folks to keep the "weird kid" at home more. But instead, she asked if it would be alright if they hired me.

I think there might have even been a little...

"He's here all the time anyway.
We might as well put him to work."

My parents said yes, and I just about exploded.

At 13... I'd gotten my Dream Job.

I couldn't believe it.

I loved it.

I started to "officially" work at the shop doing various odd jobs. Marty and I very quickly realized that I was not a good mechanic, (Seriously... I was dangerous with a wrench!) But we also figured out I was a natural on the sales floor. I loved asking questions. I loved talking with people about bikes. I loved doing research and staying on top of new products.

So it was a great fit and I thrived.

Then one year later... I was introduced to my first "hidden back door."

Marty decided to take the assistant manager and me

to a sales seminar hosted by the Schwinn Bicycle Company. It was held in Minneapolis, so after we closed the shop on a Friday night, we drove up to the Twin Cities to attend the weekend workshop.

I didn't know what to expect but when we walked into the room on the Saturday morning, it wound up being me (at 14 years old) and a bunch of middle-aged bike shop owners. I think the other attendees were a little surprised but Marty introduced me to the rest of the room in a way that made me feel like I deserved to be there.
I smiled, said "Hello" (Yeah... as I did... my voice cracked). Then, I settled in to learn.

I was still in middle school, so I was very familiar with a classroom setting. But this was different. The chairs and tables were set up in a U formation. It was obvious we were going to be listening and taking some notes, but I got the feeling we were also going to be getting up and moving around.

Doing stuff.

Within a minute or two, the trainer walked into the room and greeted everyone. He started to teach but he also asked questions and engaged the room. He was offering strategies, but he was also drawing ideas from the audience. The trainer even asked me...

the punk teenager... for my input. I can say... I learned a lot from the teaching... but the most important thing that happened is that seminar helped me to see a whole new world that I didn't even know existed.

I didn't know it at the time... but the seeds of a new Dream Job got planted on that cold weekend in Minneapolis.

When we returned to the bike shop... I still loved working there. But a new passion started to grow. Instead of just reading about bikes... I started to pick up books about selling, building trust and adult learning strategies. (I told you... I was a weird kid!) I started to find places to turn around and teach others. In fact, as our staff grew in size, even though I was still just a teenager, Marty eventually had me train our new employees on how to sell and take care of customers.

Fast forward a few decades. Now I'm in my current Dream Job of writing, speaking and facilitating events and although it looks different than what I did at the bike shop... I know the seeds for what I do now were planted back at that first workshop I attended as a 14-year-old.

That seminar was a hidden back door for me

because I didn't even know that type of work existed when I pursued my Dream Job of working at the bike shop. But I found it and I was able to walk through it... and it opened up new possibilities.

One of Sara Haines' hidden back doors was stepping in front of the camera to interview the musician coming off stage. She had prepared but that type of opportunity hadn't existed before that very moment. It only came because she was in the throes of her current work. It had been hidden up to that point. But when she found it... she walked through it... and it opened up new opportunities.

John Morgan's hidden back door came when he started to receive phone calls asking for his advice. Initially, he began to research marketing and branding in order to sell more houses. But unlike the classes he'd taken in school, in this case, he loved reading and learning. These concepts stuck with him. He just seemed to understand them. Business strategies just started to pour out of him and he loved it. When he started in real estate, being a branding consultant wasn't even on his radar. But once he started to walk through that hidden back door... he found an entirely new Dream Job that fit like a glove.

I mention the "Hidden Back Door" concept for a number of reasons.

If you're still feeling stuck because you're not 100% sure what your next Dream Job is... START anyway.

There's a very good chance you'll figure it out as you go.

Plus, even when you find a Dream Job... there's a REALLY good chance you'll be introduced to other Dream Jobs through a hidden back door.

> *"Faith is taking the first step even when you don't see the whole staircase."*
> - Martin Luther King, Jr.

Begin.

Don't wait.

If you're not in a Dream Job yet... that's okay.

Get intentional.

Either find a Bridge Job or turn your current work into a Bridge Job.

> *"If you don't go after what you want, you'll never have it. If you don't ask, the answer will always be no. If you don't step forward, you're always in the same place."*
> - Nora Roberts

If you're currently in a Dream Job... awesome.

Keep at it.

Bring excellence.

Have fun.

Love and serve people well.

Help others to achieve their's.

Look for a hidden back door as you do.

If you've had a Dream Job... but it's lost it's luster... or it went away... Recommit. Dig in.

There are more Dream Jobs out there.

It's a new season.

Begin again.

And hey... no matter what... dream bigger.

Don't commit to just having one Dream Job in your lifetime. Commit to a career where you have a multiple Dream Jobs...

Commit to a journey to finding work that you love and/or work that enables you to do something you love.

NOTES:

Conclusion

I'll admit it.

There's a part of me that hopes you don't make it to this chapter.

Why?

Well... my hope is that you get so caught up in the process we've been exploring together that you almost forget to read this last short chapter.

You dig in. You go after it.

You start:

- Choosing the right attitude
- Maximizing Bridge Job opportunities
- Looking for clues to clarify your passions
- Creating lists of dreams for your life
- Conducting experiments to build momentum
- Being willing to fail from time to time
- Setting magnetic goals that excite you
- Asking for help (and giving some help too)
- Being intentional as you move forward
- Committing to having multiple dream jobs

You redefine what a Dream Job is to you... and you go out and either create one or get one.

But hey... I know you.

You are a finisher.

OF COURSE... you're going to read this chapter.

Because you get things done.

That's just who you are.

So... I want to say GREAT WORK!

Well done for digging in.

Heck, well done for even picking up a book on the subject of dream jobs! In this cynical and skeptical world... it would be easy to totally dismiss the concept and poo poo it as something that's silly to pursue. (Yeah... I just said "poo poo.")

BUT again... that's not you.

You believe dream jobs are possible.

They're real.

I'm guessing that all the stories of real people like Sara, Diego, John, Antonio, Lise and others simply confirmed something you already knew deep down inside.

Dream Jobs exist.

They're not easy.

They're not without challenges.

But they are out there.

And there's at least one with your name on it!

I'm also betting that the strategies we've talked about didn't necessarily surprise you... but instead... they helped to reinforce things you already knew in your heart of hearts.

Am I right?

I'm betting so.

You're one smart cookie.

You know this stuff.

Now... go out and do it.

Start.

Whether you're 13, 23, 43 or 73.

Start.

As you do... remember: You haven't missed it.

You're not too late.

Start where you are.

Keep that old Chinese proverb in mind that says:

> *"The best time to plant a tree was 20 years ago.*
> *The second best time is right now."*

NOW is your best time to start.

Go find or create your next dream job.

And PLEASE... keep me in the loop as you do... so we can inspire the world to go after more dream jobs... through telling YOUR story too!

I NEED YOUR HELP!

THANK YOU!

Thanks so much for reading my book!

I really appreciate your feedback and I love
hearing from you.

Please leave a helpful review on Amazon letting me
know what you think of the book.

I LOVE hearing from you!

Thanks SO much!

- Mitch Matthews

About the Author

Mitch Matthews

Mitch Matthews is a keynote speaker, success coach and best-selling author.

He speaks to audiences around the world on the power of "DREAM. THINK. DO."

In 2006, Mitch started the BIG Dream Gathering. It began as a "happy accident," but it has grown into a national movement! Mitch and his Dream Team host BIG Dream Gatherings at top universities around the country!

He has become a well-respected thought leader on coaching and work-place mentoring. Plus, he has created a coach-training program that has been utilized around the globe.

You can listen to Mitch's top ranked weekly podcast called, "**DREAM. THINK. DO.**" on iTunes.

Mitch proudly lives a "highly-caffeinated" lifestyle in Des Moines, Iowa with his wife and their two sons.

You can find out more and connect with Mitch at: MitchMatthews.com and BIGDreamGathering.com.

88561356R00130

Made in the USA
Columbia, SC
31 January 2018